Research on Preparing Teachers Who Can Meet the Needs of All Students

Teacher Education Yearbook XI

Edited by

Julie Rainer Dangel and Edith M. Guyton

KENDALL/HUNT PUBLISHING COMPANY
4050 Westmark Drive   Dubuque, Iowa 52002

Teacher Education Yearbook XI

EDITORS

Julie Rainer Dangel, *Georgia State University, Atlanta*
Edith M. Guyton, *Georgia State University, Atlanta*

EDITORIAL ADVISORY BOARD

Violet Allain, *James Madison University*
David M. Byrd, *University of Rhode Island*
Angela Case, *University of Delaware*
Nancy Dana, *Penn State University*
Emma Savage-Davis, *James Madison University*
Joyce Garrett, *Boise State University*
P. Rudy Mattai, *SUNY College at Buffalo*
Gwendolyn Middlebrooks, *Spelman College*
D. John McIntyre, *Southern Illinois University*
Sandra J. Odell, *University of Nevada–Las Vegas*
Mary John O'Hair, *University of Oklahoma*
Diane Silva, *University of Florida*
Melba Spooner, *University of North Carolina in Charlotte*
Edwina Batle Vold, *Indiana University of Pennsylvania*

EXECUTIVE DIRECTOR

Lynn Montgomery, *Association of Teacher Educators, Reston, Virginia*

Contents

Foreword

Carrie Robinson is Professor of Literacy Education at New Jersey City University (Jersey City, New Jersey) and President of the Association of Teacher Educators (ATE). A member of ATE since 1989, she served on ATE's Board of Directors, is a member of the ATE Multicultural Education Special Interest Group serving as the SIG's Chair and Vice Chair. Dr. Robinson was a member of two commissions: Gender Equity in Teacher Education and Constructivist Teacher Education, was former chair of Fiscal Affairs Committee, has been on two national conference planning committees, and was the recipient of an ATE Presidential Service Award in 1996.

Teacher Educators Leading the Challenge for Academic Excellence in the 21st Century

It does not matter what children bring to school.
What matters most, is what teachers do with
what children bring to school.
Ronald Edmonds

I n addition to the aforementioned quote, the late Ronald Edmonds also left behind the legacy of recognizing that all children can learn. With this legacy, the challenge for educators becomes what can children learn, under what conditions can they learn it, and in what sequence can they learn it? Please note that it is not defined in this Foreword. It varies within classrooms (P–12 and post-secondary) and across educational institutions (P–12 and post-secondary). Additionally, the educational standards regarding teacher, candidate, and student achievement are currently at the forefront of discussions on national, state, and local levels. This dialogue is also heavily embedded in the accreditation process within the education community. Therefore, the education community continues to discuss what constitutes teacher and student achievement and how do we effectively measure educational quality.

Diversity and pluralism are and will be the hallmarks of schools and society in the 21st century. Students and teachers who represent diverse cultural backgrounds characteristic of this pluralism are and will be in our schools and classrooms, public and private, striving to develop their abilities, interests and skills. This diversity places and will continue to place great demands and challenges upon teacher educators, teachers, and other school personnel in the quest to ensure that all students. Working collaboratively with P–12 students, candidates, parents, teachers, teacher educators, other school personnel, and politicians (who exert tremendous influence (and resources) over what happens in all schools today), we must reform and transform schools to create classrooms and school settings that prepare all students for careers and life in our increasingly complex and technological international society, sometimes referred to as the global village.

All public educational institutions pledge to ensure *equal educational opportunity* for all learners. In our global village, the *equal educational opportunity* pledge poses the challenge of providing academic excellence for diverse learners and teachers. Today's educational climate calls for critical examination of educational outcomes and holds teachers and teacher educators accountable for P–12 student and/or candidate outcomes. Therefore, it is imperative that teacher educators engage in the on-going dialogue that adds to the professional's knowledge base of instructional practices and fosters culturally responsive pedagogy. The research on quality teaching and learning should inform what we do in our classrooms. It is most unfortunate but true. The educational community aids some learners in their quest to become literate individuals who can effectively enhance the quality of our democracy. Other learners appear to learn in spite of and despite the obstacles that they must overcome within and outside of the educational system that has pledged to provide a first class education to every child.

If our education system is ever to accomplish the goal of leaving no child behind, our system cannot leave a single candidate, a single teacher, a single member of the school community of learners, or any teacher educator behind! Toward the goal of fostering an academic community that engenders success for all learners as well as facilitators of learning, teacher educators should lead the discussion and help others grapple with the role of diversity in the debate about the alignment of educational standards and outcomes.

ATE strives to be a vocal advocate for academic excellence for teacher educators, teachers, candidates, and P–12 students, rigorous academic content for all students and candidates, and the development of supportive educational environments that enable all learners to succeed academically. In this period of grave concern regarding teacher quality and student achievement, this eleventh edition of the ATE yearbook series presents research in three broad areas: preparing educators to work with all children, preparing educators to work in urban school, and educators working in culturally diverse schools. If we are truly to make a difference in the life of every child, our focus must be on how to ensure that every child leaves the educational system with the values, skills and abilities to think critically and to utilize knowledge to improve the quality of life for our common good. We should enhance our research base about the skills, knowledge, and dispositions that candidates need to work with all children and acknowledge that working within the urban community and/or culturally diverse settings poses unique challenges that can only be addressed by putting them at the center of the debate on quality teacher and student achievement.

The continuation of the Ronald Edmonds quote, *All children can learn,* includes *We can whenever and wherever we choose successfully educate all children whose education is of interest to us. The question is if we have the will to do it.* The authors included in this edition have responded to the challenge to explore not only what we are doing to educate all children but also whether or not what we are doing is effective. Your willingness to explore the issues around quality teacher and student achievement raised in this Yearbook denotes your commitment to advance the agenda of teacher educators meeting the challenge of academic excellence to foster teacher and student achievement in the 21st century.

REFERENCE

Edmonds, R. (1979, October). Effective Schools for the Urban Poor. *Educational Leadership*, 15–24.

Introduction

Julie Rainer Dangel

Edith M. Guyton

Julie Rainer is an associate professor in Early Childhood Education and currently coordinates the Educational Specialist Program at Georgia State University. Her research interests include teacher development, constructivist theory and mathematics education. She has published articles in a variety of journals including *Action in Teacher Education, The Journal of Teacher Education,* and *Teaching and Teacher Education.* She is currently a member of NCATE Board of Examiners.

Edi Guyton is Associate Dean of the College of Education, Georgia State University. In that position, she is the Director of the Metropolitan Atlanta P–16 Community Council. Dr. Guyton is a Professor of Early Childhood Education. She recently served as President of the Association of Teacher Educators. Her scholarship and publications are in the areas of teacher education, constructivist teacher education, and multicultural education. She was an editor of the *Handbook of Research on Teacher Education* (Macmillan, 1996). She is the editor of the Association of Teacher Educators Standards for Field Experiences in Teacher Education (2000).

Teacher Education Yearbook XI: Research on Preparing Teachers Who Can Meet the Needs of All Students provides teachers and teacher educators with current research and practical guidelines for implementing research on the issues inherent in this critical and often debated topic. The yearbook serves to inform and guide teachers and teacher educators on complex issues and provide researchers interested in teacher education with current research in the area addressed by the yearbook.

The conceptual framework of the yearbook is based on a triadic definition of scholarship: the production of knowledge, the interpretation and synthesis of knowledge, and the application of knowledge. Each year, research reports based on a significant topic are solicited for publication in the yearbook. All research reports are blind reviewed and two or three reports in multiple divisions are published. A responder, a recognized scholar in the field, reacts to the papers selected for each division. The responder synthesizes, interprets, and applies results drawn from the selected research papers. By providing interpretations and possible application of research, as well as the research report, the Yearbook raises questions and generates rich conversation around issues often surrounded in silence.

The call for research papers for this edition invited educators to submit research reports on the topic of preparing teachers who can meet the needs of all students. In teacher education today, the emphasis is on educating teachers who are willing and able to work to make all students successful. Education is a right not a privilege. The right to learn will not be possible for many people unless teacher education supports it. The Education Trust (1996) reported data to show that education improves lives and that poor people have much less access to good education. Data also show lower levels of performance among poor students and minorities. The report attributes these performance lags to teaching quality. The reports of the National Commission on Teaching and America's Future (NCTAF, 1996, 1997) confirm these data and make ties explicitly to teachers in the schools and teacher education. The reports cite many studies that show that teaching expertise influences student learning.

Yearbook XI focuses on research on how to educate teachers to teach all the students in the diverse schools of today, including work in urban schools and culturally diverse settings. Within the three divisions, authors address a variety of issues illustrating the complex nature of both teaching and learning from diverse students. For example, you will read about changing demographics, optimizing learning for all children, equity and inequities in education, recruitment and retention, the importance of reflective and social dialogue in learning, inquiry and problem solving as scaffolding experiences, and advocating for children of varying abilities with different cultural and linguistic backgrounds.

In Division I, preparing educators to work with all children, Zokaiewicz, Haynes Writer and Chavez Chavez discuss conceptualizing and practicing multicultural education, both consciously and unconsciously. The study by Stallworth, Crawford, Crumpler and Lenski reminds us of the effect of the society on a school's culture as it examines pre-service teachers' opportunities to acquire cultural knowledge. Collier and Meyers propose that teachers who engage in problem-based inquiry and reflection can accommodate the individual needs of children. Garrett links the issues identified in these chapters in her discussion of the reality of and context for preparing educators to work with all children.

In Division II, preparing educators for work in urban schools, Alder reviews the literature to reveal five areas of essential facets of educating teachers for work in high poverty schools. Lombardi, Burstein, Smith and Cunningham describe efforts to enhance the recruitment, preparation, and retention of teachers to serve diverse urban learners. Watson and Savage-Davis connect these issues in their discussion of the roles teachers play in addressing the social, economic and cultural factors that make work in urban schools a complex endeavor.

In Division III, which focuses on educators working in culturally diverse schools, Tate, Anstrom and Sanchez explore the needs of mainstream teachers working with English language learning (ELL) students. Alder's examination of "beat the odds" elementary schools indicates that the presence of both school-wide mechanisms of support and sound classroom instruction are necessary to produce high level reading performance. The study by Leidel-Rice suggests the importance of analyzing our programs from a multicultural perspective. Vold and Pattnaik respond to these papers by discussing the issue of class, the importance of collaboration with schools, and systemic reform to promote more effective preparation of teachers.

We often look to research for answers to theoretical and practical questions. However, this topic cannot be sufficiently addressed in a single study, a single chapter or even a single book. It is a topic that requires continual examination and engagement. As Vivian Paley (1995) suggests in *Kwanza and Me: A Teacher's Story,* you have to continue the dialogue; "communication has no end and there is always another story to be told" (p. 140). She further reminds us that we need diverse people in our schools so that there is a dialogue.

In the spirit of scholarship described above, the editors of *Teacher Education Yearbook XI* believe this edition raises questions, exposes ideas, and contributes to the dialogue and current research including its interpretations and its possibilities for application in the important and evolving field of inquiry on meeting the educational needs of all our students.

ACKNOWLEDGMENT

As editors, we would like to acknowledge that this work was made manageable and enjoyable by the participation of Amy Nesmith. Her organizational skills and attention to detail are a valuable contribution to the edition.

REFERENCES

National Commission on Teaching and America's Future (1996). *What Matters Most: Teaching for America's Future.* New York: Author.

National Commission on Teaching and America's Future (1997). *Doing What Matters Most: Investing in Quality Teaching for America's Future.* New York: Author.

Paley, V. (1995). *Kwanza and Me: A Teacher's Story.* Cambridge, MA: Harvard University Press.

Division 1

1

Preparing Educators to Work with All Children

Overview and Framework

Joyce Lynn Garrett

Joyce Lynn Garrett is Dean of the College of Education and Professor of Elementary Education and Specialized Services at Boise State University. Her interests include classroom management and the application of technology in educational settings. Her publications appear in national and regional journals. She serves on the ATE Task Force for Diversity in the Teaching Force.

A recent summit held in Washington D.C., Losing Ground: A National Summit on Diversity in the Teaching Force, addressed the critical shortage of ethnically, racially, and linguistically diverse teachers in the schools across this nation. The purpose of this summit was to explore both the barriers that keep qualified candidates from diverse backgrounds out of the teaching profession and to develop an action plan that will significantly reduce or eliminate those barriers. Keynote speaker, Jacqueline Jordan Irvine, opened the conference with a discussion of what she called "a culturally relevant pedagogy." She suggested that the best learning depends on building a socio-cultural context that incorporates students' verbal communication patterns, non-verbal communication patterns, and preferred ways of learning. She went on to present evidence that students learn best when instructional examples, student engagement, and assessment are contextually based and accommodate learners with special needs. Her conclusion was that teachers of color, who bring culturally based pedagogy to students of color, would positively influence the overall achievement of those students.

The reality, however, is that persons of color have a broader range of career choices today than they have ever before; as a result, too few of them are electing to enter the teaching profession. In addition, there is a plethora of obstacles that keeps them out of the teaching workforce. Some examples from a list prepared by Association of Teacher Educators Task Force on Diversity in the Teaching Force (n.d.) are: (a) failure of persons of color to graduate from high school; (b) inadequate preparation at the secondary school level; (c) greater reliance by colleges and universities on single test scores for admission to their programs; (d) lack of access; (e) lack of academic and social support; and (f) low salaries. Because persons from under-represented groups do not select teaching as a career, the teachers in American schools continue to be predominately white, [able-bodied] females, from the middle class (Applied Research Center, 2000; National Commission on Teaching and America's Future, 1996). This fact presents many challenges for those professional educators who prepare teachers to work with the increasing population of students from diverse backgrounds and students with special needs.

Teaching all of America's teachers to work with all of America's children and youth is not a new challenge, but it is a challenge that grows more complex with each passing day. As the diversity of our K–12 student population increases and the diversity of our teaching workforce decreases (Yasin, 2001; Chase, 1999; National Center for Education Statistics, 1997) it is more critical than ever that we find ways to assure that all children are able to realize their personal intellectual, social, physical, and emotional potential. Although we have come a long way toward incorporating the suggestions offered in *Diversity in Teacher Education: New Expectations* (Dilworth, 1992) and similar works, the chapters that follow clearly demonstrate the on-going need for teacher educators to pay due diligence to the fact that exposure to the concept of diversity alone is insufficient to assure pre-service candidates' ability to work with the diverse population of learners they will encounter over the lifetime of a career in education.

In the mid-nineteen seventies and early eighties many writers focusing on special education issues suggest that teachers' acceptance of students with special needs would not be accomplished without direct exposure to them. These highly respected special education professionals make it clear that a textbook introduction to disabling conditions and the presentation of pedagogical solutions to students' learning and behavior problems is insufficient to assure that teachers would be responsive to the special needs of learners with disabilities. Most suggest that any teachers' ability to work with special needs populations required a specialized set of knowledge, skills, and dispositions. For teacher education candidates who do not come with the requisite dispositions, they wrote, only extended contact with special needs students is likely to change their attitudes and beliefs.

McDiarmid and Price (1993) report the same phenomenon as it relates to socially and culturally diverse learners. They summarize the results of a three-day workshop, intended to influence participants', views this way:

> . . . multicultural presentations had little effect on students' beliefs about the capabilities of learners labeled "high" and "low" ability, about the use of stereotypes in making teaching decisions, or about providing genuinely equal opportunities to learn challenging and empowering subject matter (p. 32).

They also suggest that teacher educators responsible for preparing teachers to work with diverse student populations might need to reexamine both the content and pedagogy used by them to teach pre-service teachers about working with socially and culturally diverse learners.

In her book, *Why Are All the Black Kids Sitting Together in the Cafeteria*, Beverly Daniel Tatum (1997) did not explicitly suggest that cross-cultural contact is essential to developing one's sense of racial identity. She did allude, however, to the idea that such contacts do have the power to affect an individual's perceptions and beliefs. Furthermore, Tatum, among others (see for example, Sleeter & Grant, 1994 and Banks, 1988), points out the difficulties faced by individuals who elect to explore their own or others' racism. She suggests that this is an undertaking not easily accomplished on one's own; in fact, she notes frequently the power of continuous, guided dialogue and provides many examples of how group work contributes to a fuller understanding of one's own racial identity and that of others. It is easy to conclude from her work, that the self-awareness of teacher educators about their own racial identity, racism, and the context of cultural differences is essential in order to help bring meaning to the experiences of their teacher education students. The chapters by Zozakiewicz, Haynes Writer, and Chavez Chavez and Stallworth, Crawford, Crumpler, and Davis Lenski confirm this notion.

It has been said that a teacher cannot take a student where the teacher him/herself cannot go. This seems to be especially true when one speaks of preparing teachers to work with diverse groups of children. Each of the chapters in this division describes the critical role played by teacher educators and mentor teachers (cooperating teachers) in constructing activities, posing questions, and responding to pre-service teachers' reflections about their classroom encounters with students who are different from themselves. If teacher educators are to reach beyond superficiality in their efforts to educate candidates to work with diverse student populations, it seems only reasonable that they would need to be aware of their own attitudes, beliefs, and perceptions. While this may appear to be both obvious and simplistic, it is important to note that the authors of the three chapters in this division, in one form or another, address concerns about the need to "disrupt and transform [their own] perceptions and practices" (Zozakiewicz, et al.). Other writers, as well, discuss the requirement of teacher educators to engage their students actively in examining the foundations of their practice in order to build understanding and experience cognitive growth.

For an example, in the 1998 edition of this yearbook, Edith Guyton, writing about teacher cognition and constructivist teacher education stated:

> The work of Vygotsky (1978), Blumer (1969), and others underscores the centrality of social interaction in learning to teach. Vygotsky defined the "zone of proximal development" as the level at which a person can perform intellectually with the support of a more competent person. The expert scaffolds the novice's development by sensitively adjusting the levels of support to the novice's emerging understanding. This conception clarifies the importance to teacher education of meeting the teacher where he or she is. Vygotsky emphasized the importance of learning as a social interaction, which includes discussion, reflection, and growth (pp. 2–3).

She goes on to explain that

> cognitive development is not automatic . . . growth does not happen as a result of age or experience; it requires a stimulating and supportive environment along with appropriate interaction (King & Kitchner, 1994; National Center for Research on Teacher Education (1991). These studies strongly suggest that intervention is needed to promote teachers' cognitive growth. There must be ways of drawing meaning from experience (p. 3).

The chapters in this section are grounded in constructivist theory and provide insights into the complexity of preparing teacher education candidates for work in diverse classroom settings. Zozakiewicz, Haynes Writer and Chávez Chávez used a case study approach to examine how the conscious and unconscious multicultural practices of new teachers change over time, when they receive mentoring and engage in active dialogue about their pedagogy; Stallworth, Crawford, Crumpler, and Davis Lenski used the video film, *The Color of Fear*, as a vehicle to encourage pre-service teachers in their study to reflect on beliefs, perceptions, and behaviors as they related to cultural differences. They found that participants' dispositions were positively affected by listening to the cultural experiences of "others." The chapter by Collier and Meyers shifts the reader's focus from multicultural concerns to issues of diversity related to cognitive development and disabling conditions. The unique approach these authors use to examine pre-service teachers' development of knowledge, skills, and dispositions as they relate to and affect the instruction of young, cognitively diverse learners is to engage candidates in specific scaffolded research activities. This strategy is an excellent example of the application Vygotsky's theory of learning.

Together, these three chapters describe a number of ways, including the careful selection and application of course materials and activities, reflective dialogue, mentoring, and research-based inquiry, that pre-service teachers can become more aware of their own praxis related to teaching a diverse classroom of students. It is clear from the work presented by these authors that it is possible to develop the sensitivity of pre-service students, regardless of their own race, ethnicity, or state of able-bodiness, to the culture and individual needs of students whom they teach. It also is evident that it is possible to do this in ways that ensure the greater likelihood that every child will benefit fully from his or her school experience.

REFERENCES

Applied Research Center. (2000). *Facing the Consequences: An Examination of Racial Discrimination in U.S. Public Schools.* Washington, DC: Author.

Association of Teacher Educators Task Force on Diversity in the Teaching Force (n.d.). *Diversifying the Teaching Force at the Dawn of the 21st Century: An Imperative for a Democratic Society.* Unpublished manuscript. Reston, VA: Author.

Banks, J.A. (1988). *Multiethnic Education: Theory and Practice (2nd Ed.).* Boston: Allyn and Bacon, Inc.

Blumer, H. (1969). *Symbolic Interactionism: Perspective and Method.* Englewood Cliffs, NJ: Prentice Hall.

Chase, R. (1999). Untitled introduction to web page. Washington, DC: National Education Association.

Dilworth, M. E. (1992). *Diversity in Teacher Education: New Expectations.* Washington, DC: American Association of Colleges for Teacher Education.

Guyton, E. (1998). Teacher Cognition, Constructivist Teacher Education, and the Ethical and Social Implications of School: Overview and Framework. In D.J. McIntyre and D. M. Byrd (Eds.). *Strategies for Career-Long Teacher Education: Teacher Education Yearbook VI* (pp. 1–9). Thousand Oaks, CA: Corwin Press.

McDiarmid, G. W. and Price, J. (1993). Preparing Teachers for Diversity: A Study of Student Teachers in a Multicultural Program. In M.J. O'Hair and S.J. Odell (Eds.), *Diversity and Teaching: Teacher Education Yearbook I* (pp. 31–59). Fort Worth, TX: Harcourt Brace Jovanovich, Inc.

King, P. & Kitchner, K. (1994). *Developing Reflective Judgement: Understanding and Promoting Intellectual Growth and Critical Thinking in Adolescents and Adults.* San Francisco: Jossey-Bass.

National Center for Education Statistics, U.S. Department of Education. (1997). *Minorities in Higher Education,* Washington, DC: Author.

National Center for Research on Teacher Education. (1991). *Final Report.* East Lansing, MI: Michigan State University.

National Commission on Teaching and America's Future. (September, 1996). *What Matters Most: Teaching for America's Future.* New York: Author.

Sleeter, C.E. and Grant, C.A. (1994). *Making Choices for Multicultural Education: Five Approaches to Race, Class, and Gender.* New York: Merrill.

Tatum, B.D. (1997). *Why Are All the Black Kids Sitting Together in the Cafeteria?: And Other Conversations about Race.* New York: Basic Books.

Vygotsky, L. (1978). *Mind in Society.* Cambridge, MA: Harvard University Press.

Yasin, S. (2001). *Diversity in the Teaching Force: Summit Highlights.* *http://www.aacte.org/Multiculural/summit_highlights.htm.*

Conscious and Unconscious Multicultural Practices of New Teachers

Rethinking Teacher Education as a Reflective Circle

Cathy A. Zozakiewicz, Jeanette Haynes Writer, and Rudolfo Chávez Chávez

Cathy A. Zozakiewicz is an Assistant Professor in the Department of Curriculum and Instruction at New Mexico State University. Her research interests and publications focus upon multicultural teacher education, mentoring for student teachers, feminist poststructural pedagogies, and multicultural school reform in math and science.

Jeanette Haynes Writer is Assistant Professor in Curriculum and Instruction at New Mexico State University. Her specializations include Native American Education, Critical Multicultural Teacher Education and Native American Identity. Her most recent publications include the need for exploration of Native identity in teacher education programs and critical multicultural education.

Rudolfo Chávez Chávez is a Professor in the Department of Curriculum and Instruction at New Mexico State University. His research interests include critical multicultural teacher education and Latina/o students placed at risk. His most recent publications include curriculum narratives, border issues, and critical multicultural education with critical race theory.

ABSTRACT

Preparing teachers to become multicultural educators is no simple task as the literature attests. In order to better understand the longitudinal journey student teachers take in conceptualizing and practicing multicultural education from the beginning of a teacher education program to the final field experience, we completed case studies with three teachers. Through mentoring visits, reflective dialogues and other data sources, we began to capture and reflect upon the conscious and unconscious conceptualizations and practices of multicultural education in the field. The research findings indicated that multicultural mentoring had a positive impact on the development of more conscious understandings and practices of multicultural education for teachers. Mentoring and dialoguing about the cases provided us, as teacher educators, with insights into how to rethink our own practices for helping students develop more complicated articulations of multicultural education. Creating such a reflective circle of research and practice evokes new possibilities.

As multicultural teacher educators of diverse backgrounds,[1] we work in the cultural borderlands of the Southwest. We are charged with preparing our students to be effective and successful multicultural teachers within and beyond this particular cultural borderscape (Chávez Chávez, 1999). Preparing student teachers to become critical multiculturalists is no simple or easy task as the literature attests (Chávez, O'Donnell & Gallegos, 1995; Fuller, 1994; Ladson-Billings, 1995). Nonetheless, we have designed a teacher education program with a critical, multiculturalist vision, a program that places multicultural education, critical pedagogy and social justice at its center. As multicultural educators and scholars, we are interested in examining the longitudinal paths our students take as they move from one end of the program, coursework, to the other, full-time student teaching.

Through this longitudinal study we continue to push the envelope of conversation and research on multicultural education and transformative teacher education programs. Whereas, much of the multicultural literature implies the notion that we "have arrived," and are doing very good things in terms of educating our students about diversity and social justice issues (Ladson-Billings, 1998; Nieto, 1996; Sleeter & McLaren, 1996), we believe that we have much yet to do. To have a more complete picture of Teacher Education (TE), coursework and fieldwork cannot be studied without consideration of the other.

As we examined our students' learning paths and practices from a multicultural perspective, we gained insights that assisted us in interrogating our own pedagogies as multicultural teacher educators in the borderscape. We sought to disrupt and transform our perceptions and practices as multicultural teacher educators in order to help our students become more committed and effective cultural workers within the contexts of schools and communities. As multicultural educators, we asked the critical question: What are we learning? Multicultural education is a process in which we must be perpetually engaged; we must examine our pedagogies, actions and reflections as individuals and colleagues in teacher education programs. Have we gotten multicultural education?

Key findings from the study demonstrate that the new teachers involved struggled initially with being able to identify, in comprehensive ways, what was multicultural about their teaching practices. Through our reflective dialogues with them as multicultural mentors, we found that the teachers involved became more conscious about naming and practicing more holistic conceptualizations of multicultural education in their field setting. In addition, the reflective conversations we held with the teachers, and with each other as critical multicultural teacher educators about the case studies, provided us the opportunity to rethink our own practices in our teacher education program. Hence, one of the key findings that this study uncovered that will be discussed within the paper was the importance of reflective dialogue as a vehicle for teaching transformation for both the new teachers involved and ourselves as teacher educators. This led us to begin to rethink the need for teacher education to be a reflective circle.

Review of the Literature

Historically, critiques of teacher education programs have espoused for decades that we still do not know the best way to prepare teachers (Conant, 1963; Smith, Cohen & Pearl, 1969). In more recent years, with the demographic shifts in the population and as the area of multicultural teacher education has grown, there are similar claims that we are still searching for the most effective ways to prepare teachers. Particularly now, educators are focused on developing programs to prepare teachers for culturally diverse populations (Goodwin, 1994; Ladson-Billings, 1995; Zeichner, 1996). This has become an even larger concern because today's demographics show that most of the teachers being prepared to teach our diverse children are white and female (Gomez, 1994; Ladson-Billings, 1995). With the increase in scholarship on what multicultural teacher education should include, there is still a large gap in the literature that studies such practice (Martin, 1995).

Yet, within the literature that speaks to multicultural teacher education programs and practices, most often studies concentrate on one course within a program (Ahlquist, 1991; Sleeter, 1996). Also, though this literature is important and rich in describing multicultural teacher education in practice, it most often focuses upon the students' responses, reactions and resistances to such courses, and seldom turns the research lens to the teacher educators' practices (Martin, 1995; Sleeter, 1996). As such, within this literature is a tone that works to construct student teachers as being deficient in terms of their abilities to become critical and multicultural educators. This often is connected to the ethnic and gendered make-up of the education students who are disproportionately Anglo and female. Very little is written about teacher education practices within more diverse university settings. These are all silences that educational scholars are calling to have addressed through empirical research studies (McWilliams, 1994). The longitudinal case studies that this research study explored addressed these silences in several ways and on several levels.

We were particularly interested in reflecting and transforming our practices as critical multicultural teacher educators through our research work together. This was in direct response to the tone of the literature that often leaves the reflections and transformations of the researcher/teacher educator as silent or less central in the multicultural literature. This commitment to rethinking our own practices through reflective dialogue connects to the work of Freire (1989):

> If it is in speaking their word that men [and women], by naming the world, transform it, dialogue imposes itself as a way by which men [and women] achieve significance . . . Dialogue is thus an existential necessity. ...dialogue is the encounter in which the united reflection and action of the dialoguers are addressed to the world which is to be transformed and humanized . . . (p. 77).

In order to transform, in order to participate in the transformation of the understandings and practices of our student teachers as multiculturalists, there must be a conscious willingness to name what multicultural education looks like for teachers and teacher educators. This study has come to represent for us and, we hope, for the larger teacher education community, the search for a fuller and more conscious understanding of what it means to be an effective critical multicultural teacher educator in university contexts and to be an effective multicultural teacher for children in diverse school settings.

In terms of how we situate ourselves within the multicultural education literature, we operate within the principles of the definition of multicultural education (MCE) put forward by Nieto (1996, pp. 307–308):

> Multicultural education is a process of comprehensive school reform and basic education for all students. It challenges and rejects racism and other forms of discrimination in schools and society and accepts and affirms the pluralism (ethnic, racial, linguistic, religious, economic, and gender, among others) that students, their communities, and teachers represent. Multicultural education

permeates the curriculum and instructional strategies used in schools, as well as the interactions among teachers, students, and parents, and the very way that schools conceptualize the nature of teaching and learning. Because it uses critical pedagogy as its underlying philosophy and focuses on knowledge, reflection, and action (praxis) as the basis for social change, multicultural education promotes the democratic principles of social justice.

Methodology

This qualitative study was conducted employing case studies of two pre-service students and one first year teacher. For this paper, only the cases of the two students who were student teaching during the spring 2001 semester will be discussed. Each participant had taken the Multicultural Education course during the spring of 1999 with one of the three researchers.

The collective case study method (Stake, 1994) was utilized to gain a better understanding of pre-service students' and the first year teacher's experiences through our TEP. Classroom observations, interviews, analysis of the participants' written artifacts, and profiles of the school and community sites composed the case studies. Additional data from an early stage of the study that investigated student attitudes and engagement in the multicultural education course also were utilized.

The researchers, who are all tenured or tenure-track multicultural faculty, observed, critiqued, and analyzed the work of the student teachers as they struggled and succeeded to move critical multicultural educational theory from their coursework into practice within student teaching. The researchers also reflected on their theory and praxis. The researchers functioned as instruments in the research due to the interactions with the students, mentor teachers and other educational personnel, and through the interpretation of the data (Denzin, 1994; Glesne & Peshkin, 1992).

STUDENT TEACHER PARTICIPANTS

The student participants, one Anglo woman, one Mexican-American/ Chicano man, and one Chicano man,[2] were chosen for this study based upon several initial criteria. First, during the fall of 2000, we, the researchers, met to look over the list of student teachers that would be completing their full-time student teaching experience in the spring 2001. We pulled files of students who had taken the multicultural education course with either Rudolfo or Jeanette within the last 2 years. Once compiled, we called those students together, explained the research project, and asked for volunteers. Based

upon interest, we narrowed a list of 6 students down to 3, according to proximity, representation from two school districts, and wanting to include a
diverse pool of students. We decided to include an Anglo woman due to the
fact that Anglo women represent a majority of the teaching population
across the United States. The other two participants, a Mexican-
American/Chicano man and Chicano man, were chosen because they were
less representative of the teaching population as a whole and from cultural
backgrounds different from that of the teaching majority. They were, however, more culturally representative of the students within our university. For
this paper, we are concentrating on the two case studies about the student
teachers, Sandy and David,[3] in order to provide a more in-depth analysis of
their development as multicultural teachers throughout the teacher education program.[4]

Artifacts and Data from the Courses and Student Teaching Semester

The analysis in this article focused on data sources collected during the student teaching semester which included field notes from mentoring observations, transcripts of mentoring conferences, participant interviews, seminar
artifacts and assignments,[5] and profiles of the school and community sites.
The study of the student teachers in the field began in January 2001 and continued through May 2001. During this time an informal observation, three
formal mentoring observations, and two interviews were conducted with
each student teacher. Participant interviews occurred in January and May
and included reflective questions regarding cultural identity, MCE understandings and practices, and their experiences in the TEP and College of
Education. Data from an early stage of the study was also utilized, yet in less
central ways.[6] These data included classroom observations, course evaluations, papers/assignments, student focus group interviews and instructor
interviews. The focus group interviews (Taylor & Bogdan, 1984) consisted of
the informal conversational and standardized open-ended interviews
(Patton, 1990).

Analysis of the Findings: The Conscious and Unconscious Practices of MCE

As we began preliminary analysis of the data, sharing and discussing our
interviews and mentoring visits with the student teachers, two conceptual

themes began to emerge around understandings and practices of multicultural education: conscious and unconscious practices of multicultural education. We noticed that there was a discrepancy/limitation to the way our student teachers were consciously *naming* multicultural education and which practices they felt they had *implemented* in their classrooms that were multicultural and what we were witnessing in our visits that they were not consciously naming as multicultural. As such, we began to read our initial findings through these lenses, conscious and unconscious multicultural education practices. The conscious multicultural education elements are those that the individual participants have the ability and inclination to name and recognize. The unconscious multicultural education elements are the practices that the researchers witnessed that fall within the comprehensive definition of multicultural education but that the student participants did not name or recognize as multicultural and implemented nevertheless.

In discussing conscious and unconscious practices, we build off Freire's (1970) ideas regarding consciousness, that is, learners' and educators' critical levels of knowing through naming and problematizing their experiences, and transforming reality. Consciousness is developed by codifying and detoxifying representations through the dialectical process. In this way, conscientization occurred for both the student teachers (the learner-educators), and for us (the educator-learners), because by examining and understanding the student teachers' conscious and emerging conscious MCE practices, we were "not only in the world, but *with* the world" (p. 28).

The following describes the findings within each individual case study as they connect to the themes of conscious and unconscious practices of multicultural education.

The Case Study of Sandy at Hawkins Elementary

Sandy, in our initial conversations, identified herself as an Anglo woman, in her early twenties, who acknowledged the less than pleasant history that being Anglo entails. In terms of her student teaching placement, Sandy worked in a fifth grade classroom with a diverse population of students from Latino/a, Anglo, African-American and Asian-American backgrounds, as well as students identified with learning disabilities and as gifted and talented. Her placement was at a large elementary school within the closest and largest school district.

Sandy's Experience in the TEP Prior to Student Teaching

When Sandy was asked to reflect upon her experiences within the TEP prior to student teaching, she had this to say about the multicultural education course she had taken at the beginning of the program:[7]

> I think that course mainly helped me, as an individual . . . discover who I was. And I think that's important, too, for anybody to be able to do that. We read articles, we talked about . . . what our history was as human beings. . . . But I feel like the biggest thing I gained was learning about myself. Not really learning how to teach multiculturally. I mean one thing we did talk about was not just singling people out. And saying, "Oh, this is important to Asian Americans," but making it part of the whole curriculum. That's the one thing that I really remember. But otherwise it was mostly an internal journey. But that's important, because [Dr. Chávez] forced us to think about stuff that was uncomfortable. Which was good, but it was hard. It was like one of the hardest classes I ever had. I think that's really important for, especially educators to know who you are, where you come from . . . (Sandy 1: 7–8).

Sandy remembers the multicultural education course being more of an "internal journey" of understanding who she was culturally and historically. She remembers these elements as the conscious part of that journey and recalls the struggles of examining uncomfortable issues, while acknowledging the importance of such exploration, especially for teachers. From her statements, it is evident that her journey as a conscious multicultural educator began within this course, where she began to read the world and her position within it in deeper and more culturally historic ways. It is also evident here, however, that she did not feel the multicultural course focused upon how to translate multicultural education into practice in comprehensive ways. Though such discussions may have happened in the course, this is not what she remembers, or what seemed to impact her the most within this experience. The internal journey of becoming conscious of cultural issues was most central in her reflections. Let us now move to how, as she began her student teaching experience two semesters following the multicultural course, she defines and begins to practice multicultural education in her field placement.

Conscious Naming and Practices of Multicultural Education during Student Teaching

During the first interview, each participant was asked to name her or his understandings and practices of multicultural education. The following are excerpts that begin to capture Sandy's conscious naming and practices of MCE from the first half of the semester. Sandy believed that:

Multicultural education means practicing equality in everything you do in the classroom . . . in the materials you read . . . adding all the histories . . . to being fair in practices, calling on girls as much as boys, Anglos as much as Hispanics. . . . It's about not just including Black history during Black History Month, and not making MCE about studying one culture, but it's embodying that all year round, not out of context. . . . In the way you talk to students and how you don't make judgments about them based on being Hispanic or of a low socio-economic status . . . and in the perspectives content is presented from (Sandy 1: 2).

When asked to name the multicultural practices that she had implemented so far, she explained:

In January, we watched a movie about Martin Luther King, Jr. and did a play on Ruby Bridges. We were not studying this because of Black History Month, but to prepare the students to talk about discrimination . . . before we read *Roll of Thunder*, which is a story about African Americans being mistreated in the 1930s. I wanted to give the kids a chance to think about these issues. It's great to know about famous Civil Rights leaders, but there [are] also others . . . that have been mistreated, such as Jews during the Holocaust or the Japanese Internment Camps . . . It's not just one group of people . . . experiencing this . . . we've all been mistreated, but what are we going to do about it as human beings (Sandy 1: 4).

Here, Sandy is conscious that MCE involves content and treating children in equal ways. She is also conscious of the fact that race and ethnicity issues must be included year round rather than only during holidays. Most importantly, she is conscious of social justice in terms of engaging in a dialogue with her students regarding discrimination and entering into talk about social action. So, in some important ways, Sandy does have a holistic idea of MCE early in her field experience.

Unconscious Non-Practices First Half of the Semester

Based upon our beginning conversations and my early visits to Sandy's classroom, the following themes arose that demonstrated unconscious non-practices of MCE during the early part of her field experience. Whereas Sandy was bringing a lot of African American information to the students' attention, she was not bringing in information that made connections to the students' own cultural and regional experiences, i.e. Hispanic, Asian

American and Native American information. She was not yet connecting her content to historical, everyday local and relevant acts of discrimination. Also, much of her content still focused upon issues of race and ethnicity and had not yet expanded to other areas of diversity, such as gender, language and socio-economic status. In addition, Sandy was not yet integrating her students' experiences and cultural resources into her curriculum planning. She was not yet consciously attending to their prior knowledges or diverse learning needs as she developed learning activities. And though Sandy had begun discussions of discrimination and social justice with her students, she was only discussing them from a place of individual accountability and action. The structural inequalities inherent in our society and talk of social action on a collective political level were still within the unconscious non-practice realm.

A STORY OF CONSCIOUS NON-PRACTICES WITHIN A LITERATURE STUDY: REFLECTIONS FROM THE FIELD

During one of Cathy's mentor visits to Sandy's classroom, another theme emerged that demonstrated conscious non-practices of MCE. Before Cathy began observing Sandy, she was already using MCE literature and content with her fifth grade students and had created journals that focused upon discrimination. Cathy visited during her literature unit on Roll of Thunder and observed the following. With this novel, Sandy had created a student-centered lesson, in which cooperative groups analyzed characters in the story and presented those characters to the rest of the class. The analysis was focused on the characters' feelings and how the characters acted on those feelings. As the lesson's activities unfolded, and Cathy walked around the room, she noticed that discussions of culture and discrimination were entirely silent within the lesson. Whereas Sandy's intent was a student-centered exploration of a culturally based social justice theme, the students never actually talked about cultural issues, instead they spoke only of feelings. Initially, Sandy had as a learning goal the examination of how different people reacted to discrimination in different ways. For example, students were to investigate why some characters got angry and lashed out while others withdrew. However, this critical exploration was not realized.

During a mentoring dialogue after the observation, Cathy asked Sandy if she had accomplished her learning goals; Sandy replied, "No." Cathy asked her what she would do differently. Sandy responded that she would have had the students act out what the characters were feeling in relation to acts of discrimination. Sandy was able to see that she did not accomplish her primary learning goal. She realized that even though one is dedicated to social justice and genuinely wants to provide students an anti-biased curriculum, one could still plan or carry out a generic lesson. We are calling these conscious non-practices: MCE practices that were consciously planned but not successfully implemented. This adds another layer of complexity to our understanding of how multicultural practices may fall short within the field. If a multicultural mentor is not present to point out non-practices, they may never consciously be reflected upon. This may be a transition point in the development of deeper and more conscious practices of MCE to which teacher educators need to more consciously attend.

NEW CONSCIOUS PRACTICES AT THE END OF SEMESTER

As the semester drew near a close, there was evidence that Sandy had grown in consciously developing and naming multicultural practices with her students. During our final interview, after completing her literature study, Sandy shared this in terms of conscious practices:

> I think the best thing was at the very end . . . we read, *Why Does the Caged Bird Sing?* And we did a poetry debate on it. I wrote vague questions up on the board. And the kids got to talk about whether they agreed or disagreed with the statements. And the kids started talking about the different ways people are discriminated against. They talked about . . . the Japanese being in Internment camps . . . there were just several different ways that I was just like, "WOW, they made the connections!" It's not just African Americans . . . or Hispanics. They made the connections to migrant workers too, which I thought was really neat, that they were able to draw all that together. I think also, just knowing what the students' needs are, special ed. and second language learners. Just trying to plan lessons that met all their needs (Sandy 2: 2).

As evidenced above, Sandy became more conscious of some areas of MCE that were unconscious non-practices during the early part of her teaching experience. She was now developing plans geared toward specific learning needs and styles. She was also facilitating the connecting of national and historical issues of discrimination to everyday local and relevant acts of discrimination, such as migrant worker issues, which are very relevant to her students' families and communities. As such, she was now more consciously aware of the importance of integrating students' experiences and cultural resources into curriculum planning and instruction. In addition, she became more student-centered in her approaches to teaching. For example, in the above discussion, she allowed the students to take the conversation in a multicultural direction. Evidence of her MC growth and the impact of the mentoring visits surfaced in the analysis of the final interview of the semester, where Sandy shared that the critical suggestions shared during the mentoring visits helped her to "become more multicultural." She explains in more detail:

> I think being part of the multicultural case study was a really good experience for me, because just having you come into the class and watch what I was doing. And every time you were so willing to give me feedback afterwards. And all the feedback that I got was stuff that I had never thought about. And being a new teacher, I didn't know stuff like that. I think you were always pushing me to the next level. How could I have made that more effective? Did I meet the objectives of the lesson I was teaching? And I think having someone come in and . . . critically look at your lesson, and giving you the things you were doing good, and telling you how you could have improved this. And just pushing me to the next level, to try to figure out how could this have been better. And I don't think that I would have gotten that with anybody else. Because [my cooperating teacher] . . . didn't give a lot of criticism like that. And neither did [my university supervisor]. I think . . . just a lot of the ideas and feedback that I got [from you] were really really beneficial to push me to the next level— to become more multicultural.
>
> [For example] when I was doing the literature study, and you had come in for one meeting, I had done the lesson, and then afterward, just the questions you would ask me, that would make **ME** think about, what could I have done to make that more multicultural. What could I do tomorrow to tie it all up, and bring the different aspects into it. I think those things are really important (Sandy 5: 11–12, emphasis in original).

Sandy's words clearly demonstrate the importance and need for critical multicultural mentoring for new teachers in the field. As multicultural teacher educators, it is crucial that we are somehow involved in the mentoring of student teachers as they begin to make sense of multicultural education within a public school teaching context. For as Sandy also made clear:

> During our classes, we learned about it [multicultural education], and different ways to do it, but I never really had a chance to practice it before student teaching. Other than just my attitude towards kids... But whenever I was student teaching, I was able to practice, by just doing all sorts of ways. . . . I think, overall, that student teaching kind of brought everything together . . . and gave us a chance to practice . . . (Sandy 5: 8).

Unfortunately, often our student teachers do not have the opportunity to apply their understandings of multicultural education until they enter their student teaching semester. In order to have a transformative impact on how multicultural ideas move from ideas to actions with children, this case study demonstrates that multicultural mentors need to be a part of the process, and that our part in that process can bring about deeper understandings about the limitations of our teacher education programs as well.

STILL IN THE UNCONSCIOUS NON-PRACTICE ZONE

As the conscious MCE growth Sandy discussed and demonstrated was encouraging and exciting in many ways, there were still some unconscious non-practices present that deserve further reflection from teacher educators. At the end of her experience, Sandy remained silent about systems of oppression and social action beyond individual acts. She also continued to center upon issues of race and ethnicity more so than the other areas of diversity discussed earlier. This conveyed to us as multicultural teacher educators that though our work has been successful in certain ways, we still have critical work to do within our TEP.

The Case Study of David at Hawkins Elementary

David did his student teaching at the same school as Sandy. David, who was in his early thirties and identified himself as Mexican-American/Chicano, was in a bilingual fifth grade classroom. When asked how he defined multicultural education, David said he defined it differently than when he took the MCE course.

> I think now it's being a lot more inclusive of different races for one, different genders, different cultural beliefs and values and being able to draw from that and kind of celebrate it for everybody even if those [of a] particular type of culture [aren't] in your class. [J]ust to make others aware that there isn't [one] way that makes education go, or a certain belief that guides education (David 2: 1).

David was very intent upon including the stories and perspectives of historically marginalized groups. This stance could be traced in its development through his MCE course response journal[8] as he began questioning his own education and whose history and knowledge was privileged in the curriculum. Although, his conscious practices and statements demonstrated the importance of inclusion of the lived experience of his students, nevertheless, this was seemingly where he stopped. David shaped the curriculum in ways where students could make relationships or connections to their lived experiences, but in his unconscious non-practice he did not build onto their organic knowledge. The privileged knowledge was the traditional school knowledge. This was "celebrating diversity" without truly integrating it into the foundational curriculum.

Whereas he wanted to expose his students to those who may not be represented in his classroom or community, the Other, in his unconscious non-practice he did not facilitate their deeper understandings of themselves as individuals. David also needed to consciously articulate his role in placing himself within the curriculum or classroom. It was evident that David had developed, through and since his MCE course, a good understanding of historical and societal issues surrounding race and identity. However, his limitations on addressing other diversities such as gender, socio-economics, ability, instructional strategies, etc., were evident.

REFLECTIONS FROM THE FIELD

Language. In his first interview, David spoke of the MCE he had seen practiced in his classroom, mostly in terms of the positive and open atmosphere as related to the use of the Spanish language. His mentor teacher was open to the students speaking, reading and writing in Spanish; it was valued, affirmed, and "natural." During the first classroom visit, David and his mentor teacher spoke both Spanish and English to the students and the students had the opportunity to communicate in Spanish when they were uncomfortable with English. At the beginning of the semester students were able to take their tests in either Spanish or English. When asked about his practice of multicultural education, David made it clear that he was following through with "what my cooperating teacher is doing" but with a twist. Addressing students' identity via language was important for David, and his MCE practice included balancing the use of the Native language and English while knowing full well that students may need to "sink or swim" after leaving this classroom for their next year of school.

> . . . [We're] trying to balance that without just saying "No, you have to do it in English now, and this is why." [We're] still just trying to nurture that native language and get them ready for what is coming next (David 2: 3).

Upon Jeanette's first classroom visit, David and the cooperating teacher were responding to the students in both Spanish and English. David, during the reading period, was reading to the students from an English language book, but would consciously translate some of the story in Spanish, and students would ask questions in Spanish and English. The next visit was somewhat different. Jeanette's visit was during math instruction and the presence of Spanish had mostly vanished. This puzzled Jeanette. Paradoxically, English was emphasized because David and the cooperating teacher were consciously trying to prepare the students to move on to mid-school where they would receive little Spanish language support. A formidable unconscious practice was the reason given for emphasizing English when engaging the students in math, because, according to David, the "concepts were easier in English." David explained he would only return to using Spanish "if [the students] are not understanding a concept and if I think it might be the language" (David 5: 1).

David knew that preparing students for their transition to a predominantly English-speaking middle school context was instrumental to their academic success, but he also fully realized the importance of nurturing native language development. David, in his background project[9] assignment in his MCE coursework two years before, wrote that his grandparents gave him the "greatest gift," which was "the ability to speak, read and write in Spanish." To disrupt the implied linguistic imperialism of this practice, Jeanette proposed that a message might be imbued in the decision to use only English in the teaching of math. She reasoned that the situation might lead students to think that only English speakers can do math or that math is a higher-level subject and is only accessible to English-speakers, or Anglos. David was truly thoughtful about Jeanette's question; he needed more time to think about the ramifications of this implicit practice. He realized the importance of maintaining and valuing the Spanish language, yet was unable at this time to consciously include Spanish language math concepts in his practice.

Ethic of Care. At the first meeting of Jeanette's MCE course two years previous, David appeared in his Border Patrol agent's uniform. The Border Patrol is usually viewed as promoting a "cult of masculinity" and, in our area, agents are known to exhibit little compassion, specifically toward People of Color. David, through the MCE course, began deconstructing the Border Patrol policies and practices, which promoted White privilege and oppression. Through his response journal his began uncovering and displaying his compassion for others.

During his student teaching, David developed and exhibited a good rapport with his students. He treated the children with great respect and love—as if they were his own. David corrected and redirected his students with agile use of care and respect whereby students responded positively. David was usually in close proximity with the students and was generous with a hug or a pat on the back. There was no difference in his behavior toward boys versus girls. Light teasing was commonly used to convey his affection for students. He demonstrated the ethic of care (Noddings, 1992) in how he interacted with his students. In one instance, a male student asked David why he was always getting on to him. His thoughtful response is captured below:

> I really care about you. In fact, over time I've been here I've really grown to love a bunch of you guys, all of you. Because I love you and care for you, I don't want you acting like a knucklehead. Because you know what? The next person you deal with may not be quite like me, and used to the funny things that you say. They may just not like it at all and so then that puts you in a bad spot . . . But someday, hopefully next year or in a couple of years you will look back and say, "Yeah, maybe it was good that he got after me so much" (David 6: 3–4).

David had certainly come a long way since he first appeared in the MCE classroom in his Border Patrol uniform. This excerpt emphasizes David's ethic of care and use of humor in the classroom. He used humor to engage, motivate, communicate with and correct or redirect behaviors. David was also very affectionate with his students; they knew he cared about them. David thought his actions toward the student were just "part of being a really good teacher," and part of creating "a really safe place for the kids to be," he did not consciously name those actions as multicultural (David 6: 3–4).

David found value in being part of this research study because of the reflection it generated in him and the feedback he received from Jeanette. Such a mentoring combination was especially important because Jeanette had served as his MCE course professor. This was a powerful aspect of the reflective circle because she knew what he was been exposed to in his coursework and they had a very good working relationship, which had continued beyond the MCE course and into his student teaching semester. David said of his participation in the study:

> Just through the reflections I seem[ed] to learn a lot about things that I was doing good, but that I hadn't really thought were multicultural . . . But I think it would be . . . great if we could have more people observing us to see that we are doing [multicultural education] or how we are doing it. But definitely, I think it affected [my teaching], for the betterment of my self and my knowledge. [I have a more] a wider view of what multicultural education should be . . . (David 6: 13–14).

Participation in the study affected not only David, but Jeanette as well. Because David had been her student in the MCE course, working with him allowed Jeanette to see how the concepts, theories and ideas within the coursework translated into practice in the classroom. In addition, by seeing David in action and dialoging with him, Jeanette was able to reflect directly on her own teaching.

This section illustrates areas of David's transformation, his conscious practices and non-practices, but also reveals areas of work where transformation still needs to occur, his unconscious practices and non-practices. Essentially, we still have work to do within our TEPs and ourselves to create transformative spaces and contexts for our students so they in turn create the best possible learning environments for their students.

Educational Importance of Study

This research study is significant to the teacher education and multicultural education community because it addresses gaps in the research literature. First, as multicultural teacher educators, we studied our students' progress from the beginning of the program where they enroll in a multicultural education course to the end of the program where they student teach or teach full-time in local school contexts. Instead of examining the journey of students in a single course, we explored the entire journey through our TEP, which culminates with how the students' conceptual and theoretical work at the university translates into actual teaching practices in local cultural contexts. For this paper, we have concentrated upon the transfer of multicultural education understandings and practices into the student teaching field and the conscious and unconscious manifestations of those connections. This study makes visible the successes and struggles of new teachers working to transform multicultural education understandings into contextualized practices within the field and how teacher educators are able to help strengthen that process. Secondly, as we worked to understand the journey of our students, we utilized this information to examine our own pedagogical and ideological shortcomings and strengths as teacher educators. As an alternative to focusing on the "deficiencies" of our students, we focused instead on how we could develop stronger multicultural teacher education practices. The insights gathered on how to improve teacher education practices in order to better prepare multicultural teachers are helpful to the entire teacher education community and fill a gap within the literature. Finally, our teacher participants represented richer culturally diversity than many other studies that focus upon predominantly White female teachers. This gives us a unique cultural context from which to speak as multicultural teacher educators.

Transforming the Process: What Have We Learned as MC Teacher Educators?

As multicultural educators, we learned many things during our journey with new teachers that will benefit our teacher education program and the larger teacher education community. We discuss two larger themes of learning that arose from our analysis, the importance of MC mentoring for new teachers and the reform potential of MC mentoring and reflective dialogue among teacher educators; the creation of a reflective circle.

First, we have realized through this research that the power of one to one mentoring should not be underestimated in the development of multicultural teaching practices in school and university contexts. Our case studies provided evidence that the presence of a MC mentor heightened the consciousness of and development of MCE practices in the field. It became clear that new teachers needed mentoring that helped them more comprehensively name and develop conscious multicultural practices. A central part of this mentoring included providing ideas and suggestions to help develop more sophisticated practices of MCE, as well as providing the space to dialogue in a reflective manner about multicultural teaching with mentors who were knowledgeable in this area.

Secondly, what this study has taught us as teacher educators is that as we critique and dialogue with the student teachers about their conceptualizations of multicultural education, and ultimately their practices, we help bring attention to the conscious and unconscious manifestations of those multicultural conceptualizations and practices. What this means to us as multicultural teacher educators is that dialoguing and working with these students allowed us to also see what was effective and ineffective within our own classrooms and pedagogies, and more broadly, our TEP. This provided us with the opportunity to make visible our limitations and future opportunities. Due to our work together during this study, we have each transformed our multicultural teaching practices in various ways.

For Cathy, as the Director of the Student Teaching Program, she began to realize the importance of structuring into the curriculum development part of the student teaching assignments a section where each student teacher was required to name how each lesson they developed was multicultural. In addition, instead of having her student teachers hand in their curriculum units at the end of the semester, she began to require that they hand in a first draft earlier in the semester. This allowed her to begin to dialogue through writing with each teacher about how they were consciously naming what was multicultural about their unit, and what they did not yet realize was multicultural within their unit, or their unconscious practices. She was also able to provide suggestions and resources to help them revise their lessons to make them more multicultural. These practices have proved to be very helpful in helping new teachers take multicultural ideas to practice in their planning and the implementation of those plans. In addition, she has also begun to provide multicultural professional development workshops for both university supervisors and cooperating teachers within local districts so that more student teachers will have the opportunity to have reflective and transformative multicultural conversations with the mentors with whom they work in the field.

Jeanette, who teaches the undergraduate and graduate MCE course, learned that she must emphasize even more the complexities and multiplicities of diversity. Ideas of "celebrating diversity" must be replaced with understandings of critical multicultural education if transformative practice is to occur. Movement beyond mere MCE content to the creation of dialogue needs to happen so teachers will understand the necessity of having their students examine their own socialization into and participation in oppressive structures and actions so as to transform their world. Jeanette saw the need to further create situations in which her students were challenged in their ideas regarding the "naturalization" of concepts such as language, gender roles, socio-economic class status, etc., versus the reality of social constructions. Students must take apart and rebuild social constructions for critical understandings rather than consciously or unconsciously perpetuating myths, which privilege certain groups or individuals. Further, Jeanette's work with David emphasizes the important of knowing each student to create what she calls "a point of contact"[10] for each so that personal and pedagogical transformation is facilitated in community. Ultimately, education is a political act. Jeanette's political stance maintains that she teaches for liberatory education, for her students and herself. This can only occur through her continuous reflection of her teaching—her continuous transformation—and the establishment of one-to-one relationships with her students.

As our work progresses and continues, we will further uncover our conscious and unconscious ideas and practices of critical multicultural education. We envision this creating a reflective circle; we view more fully where we have been, so that we can re-imagine where we are going and how to more effectively meet the needs of our students. Our findings impact our teacher education practices, which impact future student teachers in fuller ways than we had previously accomplished. Student teachers' voices and experiences are necessary if such a reflective circle of research, teaching and practice is to be created.

Our case studies demonstrated the importance of on-going multicultural mentoring throughout the student teaching experience, and its implications for transforming teacher education practices in contextualized ways. It is not only new teachers who benefit from reflective and transformative multicultural dialogue, we as multicultural educators were transformed in our dialogue with the teachers and with each other. As Freire reminds:

> Human existence cannot be silent, nor can it be nourished by false words, but only by true words, with which men [and women] transform the world. To exist, humanly, is to name the world, to change it. Once named, the world in its turn reappears to the namers as a problem and requires of them a new naming. Men [and women] are not built in silence, but in word, in work, in action-reflection (1989, p. 76).

Our naming and our student teachers' naming of teaching allowed us to transform our world and begin to name it anew. In one semester, with reflective words that led to new actions, we all made changes to become "more multicultural." Still, we wholeheartedly believe that this is not enough. Multicultural mentoring needs to continue into the first few years of teaching as well, if unconscious understandings and practices are to be transformed into more conscious, holistic and social justice-oriented practices of MCE. In addition, multicultural mentoring into the first few years of teaching might serve to combat the attrition rate of new teachers; particularly those located within diverse and socio-economically disadvantaged school contexts. Finally, we recommend that multicultural teacher educators remain in close mentoring contact with student teachers as they work to be multicultural in school settings, so that we each continue to name, reflect upon and act to transform our teaching practices, in schools and in teacher education programs. Such on-going dialogue that moves from school to teacher education and back again, creates a teacher education process that becomes a reflective circle.

REFERENCES

Ahlquist, R. (1991). Position and Imposition: Power Relations in a Multicultural Foundations Class. *Journal of Negro Education, 60*(2), 158–169.

Chávez Chávez, R. (1999). W(R)i(t/d)ing on the Border: Reading Our Borderscape. *Theory & Research in Social Education, 27*(2), 248–272.

Chávez, R. Chávez, O'Donnell, J., & Gallegos, R. L. (1995). Dilemmas of a Multicultural Education. In A. Nava (Ed.), *Educating Americans in a Multiethnic Society* (3rd ed.), (pp. 52–102). San Francisco, CA: McGraw-Hill.

Conant, J. B. (1963). *The Education of American Teachers.* New York: McGraw-Hill.

Darling-Hammond, L. (1996). What Matters Most: A Competent Teacher for Every Child. *Phi Delta Kappan, 78*(3), 193–200.

Denzin, N. K. (1994). The Art of Politics of Interpretation. In N. K. Denzin & Y. S. Lincoln (Eds.), *Handbook of Qualitative Research* (pp. 500–515). Thousand Oaks, CA: Sage Publications, Inc.

Freire, P. (1989). P*edagogy of the Oppressed.* New York: Continuum Publishing.

Freire, P. (1970). Cultural Action for Freedom. *Harvard Education Review* (Monograph Series 1).

Fuller, M. L. (1994). The Monocultural Graduate in the Multicultural Environment: A Challenge for Teacher Educators. *Journal of Teacher Education, 45*(4), 269–277.

Glesne, C., & Peshkin, A. (1992). *Becoming Qualitative Researchers: An Introduction.* White Plains, NY: Longman.

Gomez, M. L. (1994). Teacher Education Reform and Prospective Teachers' Perspectives on Teaching "Other People's" Children. *Teaching and Teacher Education, 10*(3), 319–334.

Goodwin, A. L. (1994). Making the Transition from Self to Others: What Do Pre-Service Teachers Really Think about Multicultural Education? *Journal of Teacher Education, 45*(2), 119–131.

Ladson-Billings, G. (1995). Multicultural Teacher Education: Research, Practice and Policy. In J. Banks & C. Banks (Eds.), *Handbook on Multicultural Education* (pp. 747–759). New York: Macmillan Publishing.

Ladson-Billings, G. (1998). Toward a Theory of Culturally Relevant Pedagogy. In L. E. Beyer & M. W. Apple (Eds.), *The Curriculum: Problems, Politics, and Possibilities* (pp. 201–229). Albany, NY: SUNY Press.

Martin, R. (Ed.). (1995). *Practicing What We Teach—Confronting Diversity in Teacher Education.* New York: SUNY Press.

McWilliams, E. (1994). *In Broken Images—Feminist Tales for a Different Teacher Education.* New York: Teachers College Press.

Nieto, S. (1996). *Affirming Diversity: The Sociopolitical Context of Multicultural Education* (2nd ed.). White Plains, NY: Longman.

Noddings, N. (1992). *The Challenge to Care in Schools: An Alternative Approach to Education.* New York: Teachers College Press.

Patton, M. Q. (1990). *Qualitative Evaluation and Research Methods* (2nd ed.). Newbury Park, CA: Sage Publications, Inc.

Sleeter, C. (1996). *Multicultural Education as Social Activism.* Albany, NY: SUNY Press.

Sleeter, C., & McLaren, P. (Eds.). (1996). *Multicultural Education, Critical Pedagogy and the Politics of Difference.* Albany, NY: SUNY Press.

Smith, B., Cohen, S., & Pearl, A. (1969). *Teachers for the Real World.* Washington DC: American Association of Colleges for Teacher Education.

Stake, R. E. (1994). Case studies. In N. K. Denzin & Y. S. Lincoln (Eds.), *Handbook of Qualitative Research* (pp. 500–515). Thousand Oaks, CA: Sage Publications, Inc.

Taylor, S. J., & Bogdan, R. (1984). *Introduction to Qualitative Research Methods* (2nd ed.). New York, NY: John Wiley & Sons.

Zeichner, K. (1996). Educating teachers for cultural diversity in the U. S. In M. Craft (Ed.), *Teacher Education in Plural Societies—An International Review* (pp. 141–158). London: Falmer Press.

ENDNOTES

[1] Jeanette identifies herself as Tsa la gi (Cherokee) from rural northeastern Oklahoma, Cathy as a White woman, and Rudolfo as a Chicano.

[2] These are the ways our participants identified themselves culturally.

[3] The names Sandy and David are pseudonyms.

[4] Cathy mentored Sandy and Jeanette mentored David in the field.

[5] The seminar artifacts included a MCE curriculum unit, observation reflections and student teaching evaluations.

[6] Due to space limitations for this article, we chose to focus more centrally on data from the field. Fuller case studies will be available in future publications where more space is available.

[7] The TEP consists of four semesters; the first semester involves foundations courses, such as multicultural education. The second and third semesters involve a variety of methods classes across content areas coupled with short field experiences. The fourth semester is where full-time student teaching takes place.

[8] The response journal was a required assignment within Jeanette's MCE course. Students wrote at least one entry per week responding to readings, videos, and discussions relating to MCE issues in this class or students' other classes, as well as televised or published news information. Jeanette took up the response journal three times during the semester, read each one and responded to the students' writings. This took the form of a private, one-to-one dialog with each student.

[9] The background project has students critically examine the lenses in which they view the world. The lenses may be based upon ethnicity, gender, socio-economic status, language, etc., as well as beliefs and experiences. The students wrote a 3–4-page paper and presented salient points of their background to the class.

[10] Jeanette's term, "point of contact" refers to the creation/facilitation of a learning situation for a student, which is related to something the student is already familiar with or invested in so as to produce a critical understanding.

Now I See
Understanding Culturally Diverse Perspectives

Corsandra Stallworth, Kathleen Crawford, Thomas Crumpler, and Susan Davis Lenski

Corsandra Stallworth, Assistant Professor, teaches undergraduate Social Studies Methods at Illinois State University. Her research interest includes cross-cultural knowledge and cultural experiences that impact pre-service teachers' disposition to effectively teach culturally and linguistically diverse students.

Kathleen Marie Crawford, Assistant Professor at Illinois State University, teaches language and literacy to graduate and undergraduate students. Her research is in the areas of children's literature, collaborative learning environments, and negotiated curriculum within an inquiry based classroom setting.

Thomas P. Crumpler, Assistant Professor at Illinois State University, teaches courses in reading and literacy at the undergraduate and graduate level. One of his research interests includes arts-based approaches to literacy research, and drama in education.

Susan Davis Lenski, Associate Professor at Illinois State University, teaches undergraduate and graduate courses in literacy and teacher education. Her research interests include reading and writing from multiple sources, comprehension instruction, and preparing culturally responsive teachers.

ABSTRACT

Teacher education efforts in preparing pre-service teachers for the cultural complexity in present-day classrooms and beyond are often insufficient. The preservice teachers in this study engaged in a multicultural experience that challenged aspects of their world as well as aspects of society that affect the school's culture—such as the manifestations of racism, sexism, classicism, and other forms of bias—that negate learners' cultural experiences. The multicultural course materials available to the pre-service teachers allowed them to examine various forms of inequities in society and to react to the racial experiences voiced by the "other." The study presents a profile of participants enrolled in teacher education programs and relevant research addressing preparation for teaching culturally diverse students. The findings show listening to cultural experiences of the "other" can affect pre-service teachers' dispositions to work effectively with diverse student populations and attitudes for formulating teaching skills that reflect cultural influences.

The only way to kill the ignorance that empowers racism and prejudices is to educate future generations about diversity and multiculturalism. If I can make a difference in some of my students' lives and views, I will be successful (Students' journal entry, November, 2000).

R educing levels of bias and antagonism among the next generation of pre-service teachers requires teacher education programs to focus on cross-cultural training, especially multicultural education, as a vehicle to help participants acquire attitudes, knowledge, skills, and dispositions necessary to work effectively with diverse student populations. The focus of this paper examines a cross-cultural orientation that occurred in a social studies methods course in a Professional Development School. Since the discipline of social studies is designed to prepare all students for competent civic participation, the social studies course was considered a venue for determining how the acquisition of culture knowledge influences instruction. This discussion begins with a profile of the students in the nation's teacher education programs.

Introduction

Demographic changes occurring throughout the nation are leading to a growing disparity between teachers, teacher educators, and students.

Increasingly, the nation's public school students are becoming more and more diverse, widening the gap between the teachers' backgrounds and the students they teach. The composition of participants in teacher education programs is overwhelming white, female, monolingual, and from non-urban communities (Zeichner, 1993). Most pre-service teachers receive an education in a society with a legacy of racism that permeates all aspects of society (Kalin, 1994). "Most white pre-service teachers *will be affected* or *infected* with racism or at best with an uncomfortable social distance that will make teaching—and learning problematic" (Kalin, p. 171). The instructional approach for most of these pre-service teachers has occurred through the *banking concept of education*, where students are viewed as depositories and the teachers as the depositors. Freire (1993) described education as a form "in which the scope of action allowed to students extends only as far as receiving, filing, and storing the deposits . . . with the opportunity to become collectors or cataloguers of the things stored" (p. 53). The banking concept of education remains a continuous thread throughout pre-service teachers' educational experiences, even at the university level. Their teachers are often their mirror images that often lack interracial and intercultural experiences (Ziechner, 1993). Ziechner also suggests university teachers typically have avoided implementing the principles of cultural inclusion into the classroom curricula because many lack a clear sense of their own ethnic and cultural identities. For the most part, teachers of all types adhere to and/or adopt mainstream values for an "Americanized identity" (Kalin, 1994).

When these pre-service teachers enter their teacher education programs, often they encounter professors who, due to "generational teaching patterns" (Boyer, 1994), have not transformed their instruction to match the transformation of the larger society (Boyer, 1999), resulting in a stagnation of multicultural learning. Teacher training programs are also very slow in providing a diverse teaching faculty that supports and provides pre-service teachers with cultural diversity training (Ziechner, 1993). When courses focusing on diversity are offered, "students want a recipe, a how-to-procedure for working with students from diverse populations. In reality, what they need to work successfully with any student, especially students whose race/ethnicity, language, gender, and socioeconomic status are different than their own, is to raise many questions about self" (Grant, 1991, p. 252), that is, to revisit their own life experiences. Pre-service teachers need to ". . . place emphasis on how their lives as school-aged children and citizens have been structured by race, class, culture, ethnicity, language and gender vis-a-vis those of the prevailing groups and the structure of power in both school and society" (Cochran-Smith, 1997, p. 33).

Allowing pre-service teachers to engage in self-reflection can challenge them to identify and work to transform notions they carry about the motivations and behaviors of individuals who are not their mirror images. To acquire knowledge about individuals from diverse population groups, they need an exposure to multiculturalism and multicultural education.

Multicultural Education

Multicultural education is an evolving field of inquiry focusing on educational equity, critical pedagogy and social justice (Davidman & Davidman, 2001). Pre-service teachers need to understand that multicultural education is an idea/concept, a reform movement, and a process (Banks, 2001) that challenges and rejects racism and forms of discrimination in all aspects of society (Nieto, 2000). It has as a goal the transformation of society to ensure educational equity for all it members (Grant & Sleeter, 1988). Finally, pre-service teachers need to understand that multicultural education is inclusive of all students.

Multicultural Education Approaches

Initiatives by universities to diversify their teacher education programs and efforts by policy makers such as National Council for Accreditation of Teacher Education (NCATE) to transform teacher education programs for the large pool of white, monolingual pre-service teachers has been a slow process. A review of the literature reveals various effective classroom instructional approaches that have enhanced diversity training in teacher education preparation programs. Some crucial areas for diversity training are issues relating to race and racism, learning through dialogue, cultural knowledge through case studies/ethnographic studies and narrative inquiry.

The "white ally" approach (Tatum, 1994) helps white students gain insight into racism as a system and the contradictions often created in coming to term with what constitutes a just society by exploring the development of a white racial identity (Helms, 1990). According to Helms, white racial identity evolves over six stages—Contact stage, Disintegration stage, Reintegration stage, Psuedo-independent stage, Immersion/Emersion and Autonomy stage. The initial stage is characterized by a lack of awareness of cultural and institutional racism. Successive evolving stages indicate a growing sense of whiteness as a racial identity. Once students have gained an understanding of their racial identity, new information is provided through an inquiry process to help white students construct a proactive white identity.

Pedagogical response to miseducation and dysconsciousness (King, 1997) is a praxis in which the instructor is able to model consciously the relevance of culture for learning. Tolerance and respect for students are crucial especially toward students who have not analyzed their own cultural socialization system, lack strengths of diversity, or avoid raising questions about their miseducation and cultural encapsulation. Throughout the course students continuously examine their own knowledge, assumptions, life experiences, educational ideology and teaching philosophy.

Liberatory (participatory) pedagogy (Freire, 1993) emphasizes how to think and question with little emphasis on teaching skills. The focus of teaching is on the dialectical role of the instructor and the need to make learning relevant to the student by incorporating students' backgrounds in the educational process. Students come to understand that "the teacher is no longer merely the-one-who teaches, but one who is himself [herself] taught in dialogue with the students, who in turn while being taught also teach. They become jointly responsible for a process in which all grow" (Freire, 1993, p. 61).

During case-based instruction (Kleinfeld, 1989) students review cases to become aware of the challenges associated with teaching diverse student populations. Cases enable students "to discuss openly race and class issues, reflect on previously held views about different cultures, and confront their own potential prejudices and stereotype. Cases also provide a mechanism that enables both majority and minority teachers to talk together, through the distance of the case, about issues that might be too difficult to discuss openly" (Shulman & Mesa-Bains, 1990, p. 4).

Reflective-interpretive-inquiry (Hollins, 1996) relies on ethnographic techniques for data gathering and analysis. Students extensively study one cultural group to acquire cultural and historical knowledge to overcome cultural ignorance about the specific group. They formulate a working definition of culture that helps reveal the relationship between culture and school learning and supports developing an operation model base for teaching culturally and linguistically diverse students. Learning more about the relationship between culture and school learning may lead students to question the basis of school practices.

The Immersion Experience (Garcia, 1997) focuses on self-reflection and community-based experiential learning. Students spend the school year engaging in cognitive and critical reflection through small group and self-narrative inquiry tasks. The time spent in the community enables students to learn how to broaden their cultural knowledge base by working with community experts. Students learn how to interact in more authentic ways with parents and students and how to learn about and subsequently weave into their practice information about their students, students' families and community members.

Methods

PARTICIPANTS

The study took place in a Professional Development School (PDS), a year long program for students to take coursework and to engage in school experiences, including student teaching. The PDS was located in a suburban school district that describes itself as a diverse school district as reflected in student enrollment in nine elementary schools and four middle schools. The school board, the district administrative teams, instructional and supportive staff personnel are predominantly individuals of European American heritage.

The participants in the study consisted of three males and thirty-three females, all graduates of various surrounding suburban high schools. Thirty-three pre-service teachers (hereafter, referred to as interns) are of European American heritage. Five interns claimed membership in different ethnic groups (one Korean American, one Mexican American, and two Greek American). Five female instructors provided instruction for the interns: four of European American heritage and one of African American heritage.

Three of the methods instructors (reading, science, and social studies) traveled one hundred and thirty miles from the university to this PDS site to provide methods courses within the standard sixteen-week semester. Methods courses were all day sessions. When interns were not in their methods classes, they were in the classroom with mentor teachers. The other two methods instructors, employees of the school district, provided language arts instruction and also served as the program coordinators. Their contact with students was weekly, placing them in the position of nurturers to the interns.

DATA SOURCES

To prepare interns to work effectively with students from diverse population groups, an ethnographic study project of selected schools and community sites was designated for interns to investigate. The cultural awareness orientation was presented in the social studies methods class prior to ethnographic orientation and the ethnographic study. To raise interns' levels of consciousness about themselves as well as the lived experiences of individuals who hold membership in culturally and linguistically diverse groups, various activities were presented within the social studies methods class to accomplish the goal. The data presented in this chapter describe one component: the interns' reactions to a video and the knowledge they gained about racial inequality in American society by listening to voices of several representatives from culturally diverse groups.

Interns viewed *The Color of Fear* (Mun Wah, 1997), a video produced by a Chinese film artist whose mother was murdered in the family's place of business by an African American male. The video is the producer's efforts to reduce racism by bringing together a diverse group to engage in dialogue about their perceptions and experiences with racism in the United States. The participants are all males—two Mexican Americans, one Chinese American, one Japanese American, two African Americans, and two European Americans—one who is identified as a recovering racist. This group of men spend a weekend together dialoguing about their racially related experiences in American society and the resulting effects to their personhood. The men are at liberty to openly and honestly express their opinions and share their experiences. For example: the men of color consistently infer that "whites" are responsible for the racism that occurs in the American society and that it is the responsibility of "whites" to alleviate racism. Such a format enables the men to share information about their lived experiences with a high degree of emotion that tended to come across as offensive to the majority of the interns viewing the video.

Findings

The class was divided into two groups (Group A of 17 interns and Group B of 19 interns) to view the video at different times. A graduate assistant served as the facilitator for Group A while the instructor-researcher (hereafter referred to as the instructor) observed and recorded the session to provide a non-threatening environment for the interns (Tatum, 1994). The instructor facilitated discussion for Group B. Video viewing occurred in two forty-five minute sessions. The first forty-five minute session of the video (Part I) focused on racism as white dominance and superiority. The second forty-five minute session of the video (Part II) focused on solutions to bridge racial gaps by confronting racial attitudes and practices in one's community.

After viewing the video, the interns were asked to respond to the question: "What is your reaction to the lived experiences the video participants share and in what ways might the information impact your future teaching career?" Responses were collected from anonymous Quick-write activities (Lenski, Wham, & Johns, 1999) immediately after the video viewing and cassette tapes of group discussions and class assignments (Huberman & Miles, 1994). The responses were analyzed by content analysis (Manning & Cullum-Swan, 1994).

The paragraphs reflect three ways interns perceive racism in American society as addressed and experienced by the men in the video. Content analysis of their responses reveals that interns explain experiences with racism as disbelief or denial of racial dominance (Theme I), the results of a lack of and limited knowledge about racial experiences (Theme II), and a knowledge base for acquiring effective teaching skills (Theme III).

The Theme I explanation is a disbelief or denial of racial dominance as expressed in the video. Interns were naïve about the privileges associated with being White (Tatum, 1994) and the oppression (King, 1997) experienced by these men of color. They viewed people of color as having the same privileges as whites. To the interns, everyone has the same opportunities to be successful. Hearing "whites are responsible for racism" evoked the following comments:

> This movie frustrates me because the African American men are blaming white people for everything and I think it's totally ridiculous. The entire discussion was based on the topic of racism—that translating somehow that white people [are] trying to "keep other races down" (Quick-write assignment, 9/14).

> Being a white person in this day and age, I feel that a lot of this racism stemmed from a long time ago. I had nothing to do with that. I NEVER look at another minority and treat them differently—how offended that made me feel (Quick-write assignment, 9/13).

The interns are not internalizing the impact of past historical events upon present and future behaviors. King suggests these interns lack knowledge of how oppression has impacted the development of these men and the subtle racial practice the men have experienced. They become defensive as noted in the following:

> I feel that they [men in the video] are looking for ways to prove racism exists. As much as people of other ethnicities say that whites are racist, from this video I saw that people from other ethnicities are just as racist toward whites (Quick-write assignment, 9/14).

As emotions continue to soar among the interns, their discussion centers on their disgust of racist behavior and racist practices exhibited by friends and family. According to Tatum (1994), the interns do not see themselves as racist nor do they see Whites as privileged. Accepting the realities of one's white identity and the privileges that accompany that identity can be a painful process.

Research shows when teacher education programs offer courses focusing on race, class, gender, and language differences, participants disbelieve the information, are anxiety-laden, and are confused (King, 1997; Tatum, 1994). King suggests the newly acquired knowledge contradicts the American value system in which interns were socialized. To Tatum, the interns are uncomfortable engaging in dialogue centering on issues relating to racism, classicism and language diversity without experiencing feelings of guilt. Banks (2001) would argue the interns' defensive behavior and their lack of knowledge are the results of an education within a system that has not embraced multicultural education. As these interns begin to engage in self-reflection, some resist altering their beliefs and attitudes, some struggle to identify, while most work to transform notions they carry about the motivations and behaviors of individuals who are not their mirror images.

The Theme II explanation addresses the results of a lack of and limited knowledge of racial experiences of individuals from diverse groups in the United States. Often interns hold misconceptions about those who are different from them. Only one student shared that her high school experience was in a diverse setting. Others have shallow understandings of how existing societal practices of discrimination and oppression play out in society for people of color (King, 1997).

> The video has made me more aware of how others view white people and how insensitive white people can be to races other than their own. I . . . need to work at this war [racism] no matter how hard it gets and no matter how frustrated I get by people who do not understand and do not want to understand. racism when I encounter it (Quick-write assignment 9/14).

According to Cochran-Smith (1997), "when teachers make issues of power, inequity and race explicit parts of the curriculum [they] help students think critically about the information to which they are exposed...and confront individual instances of prejudices as well as structural and institutional inequities" (p. 56). What was invisible, the existing structural inequities (King, 1997), gradually becomes visible to the interns. Supportive instructors and class assignments help to broaden cultural knowledge and sharpen interns' critical perspectives as noted in a comment shared after attending a school board meeting:

> The district says it's diverse, but there are no people of color on the Board. And there were no parents of color attending the meeting. (Class assignment, 9/26).

When the lens for viewing "self" and the world become less cloudy, the interns are able to gain an understanding of how the role of oppression plays upon one group of peoples' lives resulting in privileges for another group (King, 1997).

Moving to a new and different level of consciousness, the interns begin to focus upon their racial identity (Helms, 1990) as found in these examples:

> There are certain stereotypes that some people have toward different cultures/races. I really enjoyed hearing everyone's opinion and tried listening with an open mind. [It] allowed me to see different viewpoints from a racial perspective (Quick-write assignment, 9/13).

> Rarely do individuals openly talk about racial issues or conflicts because of personal and sensitive aspects of the topic. I did appreciate that there was a discussion of all different forms of racism, [among] minorities as well (Quick-write assignment, 9/14).

As some interns work to develop cross-cultural understandings, they come full circle in gaining an understanding of how they have acquired their biases and prejudices toward members from diverse groups (Cochran-Smith, 1997).

> White people have this way of life that they don't even know is a privilege. We take advantage of it, without even knowing it (Quick-write assignment, 9/13).

Others begin to examine who they are in relationship to others as a frame of reference for understanding cultural differences and the racial experiences of others. Cochran-Smith also suggest interns need to construct knowledge of "self," "other," and "otherness" in order to acquire skills to successfully interact with diverse learners.

The Theme III explanation addresses a knowledge base for acquiring effective teaching skills. Becoming an effective teacher to all students, these interns have come to know the importance of knowing "self" and how self-reflection can enhance their teaching (Cochran-Smith, 1997; Hollins, 1996). A significant skill acquired was listening. Listening to others enables most of the interns to look inward to examine their own discriminatory and prejudicial attitudes as in the following comment:

> I now better understand the overall issue of racism. [The] video did provide me with a new awareness of how different races may feel or experiences they

may encounter to take into consideration when teaching my students [to] embrace and celebrate diversity (Quick-write assignment, 10/11).

When teachers become aware of their own thoughts and behaviors in cross-cultural interactions, they are better prepared to respond in ways that will improve instruction and the classroom environment (Hollins, 1996). As the interns' awareness of their own thoughts and behaviors in cross-cultural interactions surfaced, they began to focus on ways to improve instruction and the classroom environment. As "caring individuals who want to be successful teachers to all children, they realize they carry baggage which may result in them making assumptions and acting on those assumptions dysconsciously" (King, 1997). After re-thinking and re-evaluating the issue, a new disposition is revealed:

> I need to be careful though. I fear that I will unknowingly perpetrate this internalized racism. I will think twice before I say something (Quick-write assignment, 10/11).

When interns continue to examine their own racial identities, Hollins maintains they will recognize that all groups historically have endured oppression. Once this knowledge is internalized, interns become more accepting of learning about students' experiences outside of the classroom and see it as a continuous process, of increasing their knowledge and understanding of the students' home culture (Garcia, 1997; Kleinfeld, 1989).

> The video has [allowed] me to [view] diversity in the classroom as an even stronger component of a successful classroom. Children from different places will [be made to] feel apart of the class as well as parents (Quick-write class assignment, 10/12).

As the interns visualize themselves in teaching assignments, they realize they are responsible for practicing inclusion to ensure all students feel accepted and valued (Hollins, 1996).

> Teachers need to try to see where students are coming from. [They] also must be sensitive to differences among students (Quick-write assignment, 10/12).

Conclusion

This study was designed to give pre-service teachers in a Professional Development School an opportunity to acquire cultural knowledge for the enhancement of instruction. Watching the video, *The Color of Fear*, brought them to a level of consciousness whereby they acknowledged the importance of individual uniqueness. For most of them, an awareness of cultural and institutional racism became comprehensible and real (Tatum, 1994). They were forced to reflect upon their own biases as they simultaneously developed their sensitivity to diverse perspectives. The viewing also enabled the interns to acknowledge that diverse perspectives will come into the classroom, and that those perspectives should be treated as valuable educational assets to the learning community. As future teachers, they began to see themselves as responsible agents in promoting multiculturalism in all aspects of their classroom program. As a result of this study, the interns' world will be different than it has been for prior generations of teachers.

Although generalizations from this study cannot be drawn to other groups of pre-service teachers, activities of this nature hold promise for a more culturally responsive teaching force for the country's diverse student population. Learning through multicultural lens can enable future teachers to "conceptualize a vision of a better society and acquire the necessary knowledge, understanding and skills" (Suzuki, 1984) to work for educational changes and to carefully develop their teaching skills to "promote democratic values and the empowerment of [diverse] students" (Banks, 2001).

Implications for Teacher Education

This study indicates that the teacher interns in this study were, in some ways, open to new ways of thinking. The results underscore the need for teacher education programs to adequately prepare culturally responsive teachers. From the data, we conclude that teacher education programs need to provide a more inclusive multicultural curriculum that is reflective of the overall society. When students' learning comes from many diverse sources—literature, textbook, media, field experiences, personal testimonies—students acquire new knowledge that empowers them to question, to validate, and to analyze assumptions relating to previously acquired knowledge as they engage in dialogue with one another (Shor & Freire, 1987). The students in this study benefited from the variety of input about diverse communities that were part of the larger study.

Second, teacher education programs need to create structural home-cultural experiences (Hollins, 1996) within urban communities that allow students " to produce their own answer, not to choose from alternatives given to them" (Guilford, 1987, p. 138). Students, especially those from the dominant group who have vested interested in maintaining a status quo, need situations that can allow them to rethink, to reevaluate, and to reconstruct society for the common good. Providing discussion about a video about discrimination, as was done in this study, is one example.

Third, since rethinking one's beliefs and attitudes is a slow process (Helms, 1990; Tatum, 1994), teacher education programs need to provide participants with mentors with cultural experiences to assist and support students as they develop their racial identities. The pre-service teachers in this study were able to identify with one or more of their instructors, all of whom provided different types of cultural awareness activities.

REFERENCES

Banks, J. A. & Banks, C. A. M. (2001). *Multicultural Education: Issues & Perspectives* (4th ed.). New York: John Wiley & Sons, Inc.

Boyer, J. B. (1994). Participant Speaking on Transforming the Academy. In J. Q. Adams & J. Welsch (Project directors). *Multicultural Prism: Voices from the Field* (Videocassette). Macomb, IL: Western Illinois University Press.

Boyer, J. B. (1999). Multicultural Transformation of the Academy. In J. Q. Adams & J. Welsch (Eds.), *Cultural Diversity: Curriculum, Classroom, & Climate.* Illinois Staff & Curriculum Developers Association.

Cochran-Smith, M. (1997). Knowledge, skills, and experiences for teaching culturally diverse learners: A perspective for practicing teachers. In J.J. Irvine (Ed.), *Critical Knowledge for Diverse Teachers & Learners* (pp. 27–87). Washington, D.C.: AACTE Publication.

Davidman, L. & Davidman, P. T. (2001). *Teaching with a Multicultural Perspective: A Practical Guide* (3rd ed.). New York: Longman.

Freire, P. (1993). *Pedagogy of the Oppressed.* New York: Continuum.

Garcia, S. S. (1997). Self-Narrative Inquiry in Teacher Development: Living and Working in Just Institutions. In J. King, E. R. Hollins, W. C. Hayman (Eds.), *Preparing Teachers for Cultural Diversity* (pp. 146–155). New York: Teachers College Press.

Grant, C. (1991). Culture and Teaching: What Do Teachers Need to Know? In M. Kennedy (Ed), *Teaching Academics to Diverse Learners* (pp. 237–256). New York: Teachers College Press.

Grant C. & C. Sleeter (1988). *Making Choices for Multicultural Education: Five Approaches to Race, Class, and Gender.* Columbus, OH: Merrill.

Guildford, J. P. (1987). *The Nature of Human Intelligence.* New York: McGraw-Hill.

Helm, J. E. (1990). *Black and White Racial Identity: Theory, Research, and Practice.* New York: Greenwood Press.

Hollins, E. R. (1996). *Culture in School Learning: Revealing the Deep Meaning.* Mahwah, NJ: Erlbaum.

Huber, A. & Miles, M. (1994). Data Management and Analysis Methods. In K. Denzin, Y.S. Lincoln (Eds.), *Handbook of Qualitative Research* (pp. 428–444). London: Sage Publications.

Kalin, J. (1994). An Anti-Racist Staff Development Course for Teachers: Consideration of Race, Class, and Gender. *Teaching and Teacher Education, 10*(2), 169-184.

Kleinfeld, J. (1989). *Teaching Taboo-Topics: The Special Virtues of the Case Method.* Fairbanks: College of Rural Alaska.

King, J. (1997). "Thank You for Opening Our Minds": On praxis, transmutation, and black studies in teacher development. In J. King, E. R. Hollins, W. C. Hayman (Eds.), *Preparing Teachers for Cultural Diversity* (pp. 156–169). New York: Teachers College Press.

Lenski, S., Wham, M., & Johns, J. (1999). *Reading and Learning Strategies for Middle and High School Students.* Dubuque, IA: Kendall/Hunt Publishing Co.

Melnick, S. & Zeichner, K. (1997). Enhancing the Capacity of Teacher Education Institutions to Address Diversity. In J. King, E. R. Hollins, W. C. Hayman (Eds.), *Preparing Teachers for Cultural Diversity* (pp. 23–39). New York: Teachers College Press.

Mun Wah, L. (1997). *The Color of Fear* (Videocassette) by StirFry Seminars & Consulting.

Nieto, S. (2000). *Affirming Diversity: The Sociopolitical Context of Multicultural Education* (3rd ed). New York: Longman.

Shulman, J. & Mesa-Bains, A (1990). *Teaching Diverse Students: Cases and Commentaries.* San Francisco: Far West Laboratory for Educational Research & Development.

Shor, I. & Freire, P. (1987). *A Pedagogy for Liberation.* South Hadley, MA: Bergin & Garvey.

Suzuki, B. H. (1984). Curriculum Transformation for Multicultural Education. *Education and Urban Society 16,* 294-322.

Tatum, B. D. (1994). Teaching White Students about Racism: The Search for White Allies and the Restoration of Hope. *Teachers College Record, 95,* 462–476.

Zeichner, K. M. (1993). *Educating Teachers for Cultural Diversity.* East Lansing, MI: Michigan State University.

Developing Pre-Service Teacher-Researchers to Meet the Needs of Individual Children

3.

Sunya Collier and Barbara Meyers

Sunya Collier (scollier2@gsu.edu) is an Assistant Professor of Early Childhood Education at Georgia State University. She is co-creator of the Developmental Cohort Model preservice teacher education program and co-directs the Collaborative Masters program. Her research interests include teacher development in undergraduate and graduate programs and international initiatives for students and faculty.

Barbara Meyers (Barbara@gsu.edu) is an Associate Professor of Early Childhood Education at Georgia State University. She is co-creator of the Developmental Cohort Model preservice teacher education program and co-directs the Collaborative Masters program. Her research about educational reform in both public schools and higher education includes shared decision-making, family involvement and teacher development.

ABSTRACT

Contemporary classrooms are diverse, and educators are required to make deliberate and equitable decisions about complex problems as they address children's varied needs and learning styles. Teachers who are intentional are best equipped to determine the impact their teaching has on student learning. We reasoned that developing a habit of inquiry would heighten novice teachers' awareness and understanding of pupil characteristics and optimize learning for all children. To this aim we provided a developmental continuum of research opportunities to 20 pre-service teachers throughout the four semesters of the Developmental Cohort Model (DCM) Program.

Qualitative methodology documented how scaffolded research experiences influenced pre-service teachers' capacity for meeting the needs of individual children. Pre-service teachers became increasingly adept at accommodating children's learning needs as they engaged in problem-based inquiry and reflection. They collaborated with peers and professionals to make informed decisions. Finally, as they progressed from research apprentice to intentional pre-service teacher researcher, they confidently implemented their own inquiries.

Introduction

Our goal as teacher educators is to prepare teachers who are able to meet the needs of all students. As we enter 21st century classrooms it is apparent that the pupils are increasingly diverse, reflecting population trends, economic conditions and inclusionary mandates (National Center for Education Statistics, 2000). This confluence of factors influences pedagogy, and educators are now required to make reasoned and equitable decisions that solve increasingly complex problems as they address children's varied needs and learning styles (Darling-Hammond & Snyder, 2000). It is our position that teachers who are intentional, who are inquirers, systematic observers, data collectors and analysts, are best equipped to determine the impact their teaching has on student learning.

The essential knowledge, skills and attitudes of in-service teachers with expertise in diverse students must be developed in *pre-service* teacher education. Because research concerning children is a viable and important means of influencing student learning, it is through research that pre-service teachers' may increase their understanding of the relationship between how individual children learn and therefore, how teachers should teach (Collier, 1999; Darling-Hammond & Snyder, 2000).

DIFFERENTIATED INSTRUCTION

Well-documented in the literature on differentiated instruction is a way of thinking about teaching and learning that includes student variance (Tomlinson, 2000). Recently, domestic and international researchers examining individualized teaching point to the need for teacher researcher skills such as inquiry, social dialogue, problem solving and reflective thinking. For example, in 1995, Tomlinson studied mid-western middle school teachers' attempts to vary instruction for academically diverse students via heterogeneous classes. She concludes that teachers need to assess student understanding *(inquiry)* and use those data to match learning opportunities to student needs *(reflective thinking and problem solving)*.

In an evaluation of a support program for implementing adaptive teaching in Dutch elementary schools, *social dialogue* became integral. Cooperation with colleagues was indicated as clearly useful by 58% of the participants; they provided each other with tips and ideas, formulated and evaluated action plans, and provided feedback to one another (Van den Berg, Sleegers and Geijsel, 2001). Pettig (2000) reports on a New York School District's 5-year effort "to guide and support faculty as they redesigned classroom instruction on the basis of students' needs, abilities and interests" (p. 14). Suggestions for helping teachers differentiate include: getting a "buddy" teacher to collaborate with and discuss ideas (social dialogue) and asking questions like "Why are we teaching this?" "Is it a key part of the curriculum?" "Will the fun activities we planned lead to significant learning?" (reflective thinking and inquiry).

TEACHER AS RESEARCHER

Simultaneous to interest in research on differentiated instruction is the renewal of interest in teacher research. The existing knowledge base includes data on practitioner inquiry from the in-service and pre-service levels. Researchers have studied master's level students (Price, 2001) beginning teachers (LaBoskey, 2001) or veterans (Cochran-Smith & Lytle, 1993). Of those who have become interested in investigating undergraduate students, most have centered on the role of inquiry in the student teaching phase exclusively (Dana & Silva, 2001; Price, 2001).

The teacher researcher movement of the last decade has resulted in a variety of studies that build the case for educating teachers who make intentional and systematic the process of inquiry about their own school and classroom work. Unfortunately, this is not always apparent; adding a course here or a project there does not foster an enduring stance about practice (Cochran-Smith & Lytle, 1999). A distinction should be made between pre-service teacher research limited to the professional practicum or student teaching experience and the developmental continuum of investigation that occurs by scaffolding research opportunities throughout a program. Acknowledging that pre-service teachers move from more self-focused thinking to pupil-focused thinking (Sacks & Harrington, 1982), it is important to situate the role of research at purposeful points throughout the teacher education experience.

SOCIAL CONSTRUCTIVISM

Considering the existing literature on differentiated instruction and teacher as researcher we created a framework for pre-service teacher research influenced by the concept of scaffolding, problem solving, and the continuous nature of individual and social reflection (Bruner, 1985; Dewey, 1933; Vygotsky, 1978). Scaffolding is the logical means of framing research experiences for neophytes. In this way it is possible to revisit questions, theory, concepts and skills which best match the dynamic nature of pre-service teacher development and to provide the continuity needed to cultivate a habit of critical reflectivity (Meyers & Collier, 2000).

According to Dewey (1933), all experience is a problem-solving process, therefore, the best approach to progress of thought is a method of inquiry that allows teachers to assess their ideas and actions (Collier, 1997). Through problem-based inquiry educators are more likely and able to meet the needs of individual students. Also central to Dewey's view is the belief that reflective thinking must be continuous (Dewey, 1933). Reflective inquiry is promoted in a community where individuals are encouraged to communicate and construct values and knowledge together (Noddings, 1995; Vygtosky, 1978). Personal and social reflection enhances how pre-service teachers construct understanding about children so they, in turn, can engage children in their own knowledge construction.

The purpose of this investigation was to describe the individual research experiences of the pre-service teachers in the Developmental Cohort Model (DCM) and how the habits, skills and attitudes cultivated by pre-service teachers through scaffolded action research experiences dynamically influenced their capacity for meeting the needs of individual children. Two research questions guided this study:

1. How do pre-service teacher-researchers who participated in the DCM develop through scaffolded problem-based inquiry and individual and social reflection?
2. How do pre-service teacher-researchers who participated in the DCM meet the needs of individual children?

Methods

The methods section is organized by the following: context, the scaffolding process, the research assignments, participants, data sources, procedures, and approach to data analysis.

CONTEXT: THE DEVELOPMENTAL COHORT MODEL (DCM)

It is important for teacher education programs to acknowledge the importance of action research experiences while also carefully positioning these experiences to demonstrate the link between research and teaching and learning (Price, 2001). The DCM (Meyers & Collier, 2000) presented action research as a strand that had equal weight to other typical components in teacher education, such as child development, pedagogy, subject area, management and philosophy of education. We believed that if undergraduates gradually were exposed to naturally occurring research experiences they would be more likely to think and act as researchers in their own classrooms. We reasoned that developing a habit of inquiry would heighten novice teachers' awareness and understanding of pupil, classroom and school characteristics that would optimize learning for all children. To this end pre-service students need to be constantly immersed in a community where they are encouraged to think, question and criticize while learning that research is an essential component of effective teaching. These characteristics cannot develop through one project or even in one semester as is often typical in teacher preparation programs. Therefore the DCM provided research experiences over time.

Scaffolding the research experiences was possible because the undergraduates in our program remain in a cohort with the same faculty team members for the four semesters of their preparation prior to student teaching. By "looping" with our students, concepts, skills, and habits were revisited and, at each point, through a more sophisticated pre-service teacher lens.

Pre-service teachers in the DCM experienced a recursive, integrated curriculum that corresponds simultaneously with multi-faceted, sequential grade level field placements (Pre-K through 5th grade; urban, suburban, and multicultural settings). The content, research experiences and fieldwork were integrated, child development issues were aligned with field experiences, and field placements were developmentally sequenced and diverse.

These pre-service teachers didn't have discrete courses but instead, a series of overlapping courses creating a set of 5 developmental modules (Pre-K, K, 1, 2/3, 4/5 and one research module). They conducted an individual and/or collaborative research project in each of 5 developmental modules prior to student teaching (Tables 1, 2, and 3).

TABLE 1

**Scaffolded Research Conducted over Duration
of DCM (Inquiry)**

Assignment	Semester	Questions
Field Notebook (Ongoing)		Faculty Qs[1] with student responses connect theory & practice; PST[2] about Qs about teaching & learning.
Focal Study (Pre-K)	Summer	How do I document the behavior of children as an indicator of development?
Developmental Domain (Kdg.)	Fall	What do I know about 5-year-olds' physical, social, moral, emotional and cognitive development?
Reading Assessment (1st Grade)	Fall	How do I document/assess reading progress of each reader and provide appropriate instruction?
IEP (2nd and 3rd Grades)	Spring	How do I design an intervention for a child with a learning or behavior difficulty?
Children Problem Solving	Spring	How do children solve problems? How do I support problem-solving behavior of my pupils?
Capstone (4th and 5th Grades)	Summer	Questions generated by pre-service teachers with a shift toward issue-based inquiry.

[1] Q = question
[2] PST = pre-service teacher

SCAFFOLDING

The teaching team scaffolded the development of sophisticated research behaviors by giving pre-service teachers progressively complex classroom-based research problems centered on student learning. The research process for each assignment included: (a) problem-based inquiry, (b) continuous

TABLE 2		
Scaffolded Research Conducted over Duration of DCM (Individual and Social Reflection)		
Assignment	Semester	Individual and Social Reflection
Field Notebook (Ongoing)		Weekly university faculty response to notebook. Weekly peer debriefing groups. Discussion.
Focal Study (Pre-K)	Summer	PST[1] (Pre-service teacher) & CT[2] (cooperating teacher); PST & cohort community.[3]
Developmental Domain	Fall	Peer resource team collaboration. PST & peers.
Reading Assessment (1st Grade)	Fall	PST & CT; PST & children; PST & reading specialist
IEP (2nd and 3rd Grades)	Spring	PST & CT; PST & child; PST & parent; PST & school personnel; PST & cohort community
Children Problem Solving	Spring	PST & children; PST & CT; PST & cohort faculty (reflective analysis of video-tape episode)
Capstone (4th and 5th Grades)	Summer	PST & children; PST & CT; PST & peers; PST & cohort faculty.

[1] PST = Pre-service teacher
[2] CT = Cooperating Teacher
[3] Cohort community = PST & faculty combined

individual and social reflection on emerging personal theories, and (c) a series of research actions (collection, analysis and interpretation of data regarding children). As each research project unfolded, pre-service teachers were introduced to and practiced research skills developing a disposition that aids them in uncovering solutions in the next project.

TABLE 3		
Scaffolded Research Conducted over Duration of DCM (Research Action)		
Assignment	Semester	Research Action
Field Notebook (Ongoing)		Weekly questions raised in class and field experience become problems to be solved[1]
Focal Study (Pre-K)	Summer	Observation; Data management, e.g., anecdotal record keeping; Document analyses; inferences; written report
Developmental Domain (Kdg.)	Fall	Library research confirms/disconfirms observations and hunches
Reading Assessment (1st Grade)	Fall	Anecdotal records; assessments (e.g. running records); analysis of assessment data; data-based lesson planning
IEP (2nd and 3rd Grades)	Spring	Observations; interviews; data-based intervention (design, implement, efficacy)
Children Problem Solving	Spring	Facilitate problem-solving environment; videotape analysis
Capstone (4th and 5th Grades)	Summer	Researcher logs; theoretical base; methodology, triangulation & analysis/ conclusions.

[1] This first assignment's research actions. The research actions for subsequent assignments in this table always incorporate the research actions that were learned in earlier assignments.

In order to provide systematic and responsive guidance to neophyte pre-service teacher-researchers, research projects were designed purposefully to align with meaningful field experiences and readings and simultaneously build a continuum of support. Incremental assistance through collaboration with veteran researchers and capable peers intentionally scaffolded beginning research efforts, reinforcing skills, knowledge and efficacy.

THE RESEARCH ASSIGNMENTS

Each research assignment (Tables 1, 2 and 3) is structured to incorporate problem-based inquiry, personal and social reflection, and research actions and is briefly described below. The Field Notebook serves as a case example of how these research features were imbedded. For more information about how the remaining assignments met these criteria please contact the authors.

Field Notebook

At the beginning of the program pre-service teachers synthesized theory and practice each week in a Field Notebook. The DCM program faculty posed questions or assigned tasks (typically 16 in each module with some required and some free choice) that corresponded with weekly themes raised in the course readings and class discussions. For example: " Look for evidence that illustrates that a four year old's cognitive development is enhanced through play. Give two examples." As pre-service teachers demonstrated readiness and curiosity they began to frame and answer their own questions. By the final module, the notebook evolved into a personal research log.

The research process began with a question (*problem-based inquiry*). The questions, in fact, were problems to be solved. Pre-service teachers selected appropriate *research actions* (e.g., collection and documentation of data) to help them answer the question/solve the problem. Each field notebook entry was another step toward solving the larger problem: how individual children learn and, therefore, how teachers should teach.

Emerging personal theories continuously filtered through the process of *individual and social reflection*. Weekly, pre-service teachers exchanged field notebooks with a faculty member who shared critical responses to each notebook entry. These responses affirmed and or challenged pre-service teachers' initial interpretations. Also, on a weekly basis, pre-service teachers orally shared excerpts from their notebooks with peers in a small group. Peers wondered out loud, listened to one another's thoughts, offered new perspectives and inevitably reflected on their own beliefs in this social forum. As interpretations were made and conclusions drawn, the next problem-based inquiry began (occasionally, focal study and individual education plan study tasks were specifically addressed in the field notebook).

Focal Study

The purpose of the focal study was to describe a child's experience within the school setting. Pre-service teachers learned how to observe children comprehensively and objectively, so that their understanding of the child guided the education of the child's fullest potential. Pre-service teachers also began to see how recommendations that are informed by data help children become successful.

Pre-service teachers observed one pre-k youngster in eight settings, documented behavior, conducted assessments, collected and annotated work samples, filled out a progress report, wrote a brief summary of the data that could be used to guide a parent-teacher conference, inform a child study meeting or add to a cumulative record and finally presented the case to a group of 4 peers and a member of the DCM faculty.

Developmental Study

The purpose of the developmental study was to engage pre-service teachers in a peer research team to describe kindergarten children's learning experiences as they were influenced by one specific developmental domain, i.e., physical, social-emotional, cognitive, or moral. Each collaborative team studied one particular area of development, gathered observational field data of children's behavior and work supported by library research on the domain. In a culminating oral presentation, the pre-service teachers described 5 year-old learners, made recommendations for effective instruction, and documented how theories and empirical studies confirmed and/or disconfirmed the team's findings.

This project extended the research work of the individual to that of a team. Inquiry skill development was scaffolded from an exclusively field-based orientation to one that added an investigation of literature, setting the stage for the next research assignment.

Reading Assessment

Since literacy is a centerpiece of the primary curriculum, students conducted a reading assessment project during the first grade module. They worked with a group of teacher-selected readers. After observing the readers, the pre-service teachers conducted running records on each reader and used these data to plan instruction. In addition they took anecdotal notes after each lesson, documenting the students' reading behaviors and reflecting upon their own instructional decisions and methods. Simultaneously, they compiled a literacy folder for each child. The pre-service teachers then reviewed and analyzed all accrued data and planned and taught a follow-up lesson. This research assignment builds on pre-service teacher-researchers' awareness of the value of collecting and reviewing formative data in the instructional decision-making process, adds assessment techniques and further supports their growing competence in planning effectively for individual learners.

Individual Educational Plan Study

The individual education plan (IEP) study builds on the observation and data collection skills (focal study), the library research and collaboration skills (developmental study), and assessment and data analysis techniques (reading project) by adding an intervention component. It also provides the opportunity to communicate and collaborate with pre-service special educators and school psychologists (doctoral students) at a simulated student support team meeting.

Pre-service teachers target an individual child who demonstrates a learning or adjustment difference (e.g., exceptionality or difficulty). Data collection and analysis lead to an intervention that includes goals, strategies, and modifications necessary for supporting the academic or behavioral needs of the identified child. Pre-service teachers evaluate the effectiveness of the intervention, and a comprehensive report.

Children Problem Solving Study

Inquiry in this project is focused on how children attempt to solve a problem. Therefore, pre-service teachers created an open-ended problem to situate their observations; for example, "Design a box that will hold 'the most' [cereal]." Children cooperated, shared ideas, asked each other questions, tried one strategy after another and checked their hunches. The activity was videotaped, analyzed in a written reflection.

Capstone Research Project

While they were in a fourth or fifth grade classroom the pre-service teachers conducted an individual or collaborative capstone research project to ask and answer a personally relevant question about teaching and learning. They developed their question, conducted literature searches, designed the methods, debriefed with a partner, kept a research log and carried out data collection. During the summer semester prior to student teaching, they analyzed and interpreted their data, did more library work, wrote a paper and presented their studies in a research conference poster format.

PARTICIPANTS

The participants in this research were 20 undergraduate students enrolled in a teacher education program in a large southeastern urban university. Completion of the program leads to a Bachelor of Science degree and teacher certification in pre-kindergarten through fifth grades. At the outset of the investigation, the participants were in their junior year. Eighteen of the students were female and five were African American.

DATA SOURCES

All of the assignments informed the researchers' understanding of the developing pre-service teacher-researchers. In addition, three served as primary data sources: field notebooks, children problem solving study and capstone research project. Benchmark interviews and exit interviews were two additional primary data sources.

Field Notebook Entries

Five sets of field notebooks (representing 20% of the participants for a total of 120 entries) were randomly selected for analysis.

Children Problem Solving Project

Twenty written reflections were analyzed.

Capstone Research Assignment

Twenty logs and final papers were analyzed.

Exit Interviews

Researchers conducted thirty minute, semi-structured interviews after the students completed student teaching. Each pre-service teacher was interviewed by one of the authors about participation in the DCM. The interview protocol consisted of ten questions. Examples are, (a) What sensibilities/skills do you think children need in order to learn and understand? Describe where these ideas come from, (b) How do you plan to ensure that learning/understanding occurs? and, (c) How would I see children learning in your classroom? Twenty transcriptions were analyzed.

PROCEDURES

Throughout the DCM, data were gathered at strategic collection points. For example, at the beginning of the program, researchers analyzed focal and developmental studies and field notebooks. Later on, they analyzed the IEP project, additional field notebooks, the children problem solving study and the benchmark conference interviews. Prior to student teaching the capstone projects were collected and analyzed and at the conclusion of the program, researchers conducted and analyzed exit interviews. This approach allowed the researchers to see how pre-service teachers acquired research skills as they also engaged in the process of learning to accommodate the needs of individual children.

APPROACH TO DATA ANALYSIS

Constructivism provides the theoretical framework for the qualitative methodology used in this investigation (Lincoln & Guba, 1985). A constant comparison method (Lincoln & Guba, 1985; Schensul & LeCompte, 1999; Strauss & Corbin, 1990) was used to analyze data from the notebooks, assignments and interviews. Three graduate students assisted the authors with coding and analysis and transcribed the audiotaped exit interviews.

Coders read through each interview and noted topics in the margin of each transcript. Each coder independently developed codes to label emerging and persistent categories. When there were disagreements, coders shared their point of view and other cases were examined until agreement was reached. Eventually the coders developed a coding manual with examples used to define each category and this guided future coding and ensured consensus. The same approach to data analysis was applied to each of the other data sources and categories were checked across data sources to see how they confirmed or disconfirmed existing themes. The authors ensured trustworthiness through their prolonged engagement with the students (four semesters), triangulation of data due to the use of multiple data sources (see above) and the constant comparison method of data analysis.

Results and Discussion

Two research questions were addressed during the data collection and analysis. In the sections that follow, we describe findings and their significance in relationship to each question. To articulate the individual voices of the participants in the DCM over time, we selected representative excerpts from the data. Each illustration is written in first person narrative to familiarize the reader with the developing teacher-researcher disposition.

RESEARCH QUESTION 1: HOW DO PRE-SERVICE TEACHER-RESEARCHERS IN THE DCM DEVELOP THROUGH SCAFFOLDED PROBLEM-BASED INQUIRY AND INDIVIDUAL AND SOCIAL REFLECTION?

Essential findings include the use of questions to frame problem-based inquiry from the beginning to the end of the program, the value of continuous individual and collective reflection related to children's learning, and evidence of the gradual progression from apprentice to intentional pre-service teacher-researcher.

Problem-Based Inquiry

In the first module, pre-service teachers studied how 4-year old children learn and develop. One field notebook task regarding the focal child project was for pre-service teachers to solve the following problem: How did the child perform the conservation of length task? What was the role of perception-based thinking in the child's problem solving approach? When documenting her child's behavior and comments, one pre-service teacher said,

> My focal child was influenced by perception-based thinking. She knew that the ribbons were the same length, yet she was unable to get past the idea that one ribbon appeared to be shorter. Another child, who was older than my focal child gave the same responses about my ribbon being shorter after I bent it. . . . They both were focused on the fact that one ribbon was longer, and neither thought about the fact that both ribbons were originally the same length.

In this first field experience, the beginning researcher observed the two children, compared the responses of one child to an older child in the same pre-k class and came to the conclusion that pre-k children are unique regarding when they construct their knowledge of length. In doing so, she demonstrated that she was beginning to use unbiased observation to support inferences and conclusions and was recognizing that individual children develop concepts at their own pace (see research question 2).

In the kindergarten module, the pre-service teachers responded to the NAEYC publication, *Kindergarten Policies: What Is Best for Children?* The students argued for or against the idea that the kindergarten year is preparation for first grade. One of the pre-service students stated the following in her field notebook:

> ... There must be a balance ... between the teacher-centered activities and the student-centered activities ... different children learn at different paces and in distinct ways. A kindergarten teacher should provide students with time for formal teaching as well as time for student-centered discoveries in which the children learn on their own and at their own pace.

In this reflective writing assignment, this pre-service teacher noted the value of combining teacher-centered and self-guided activities to promote developmentally appropriate learning in the kindergarten classroom. This was her first attempt to assimilate the relationship between instructional decisions and philosophy of teaching and learning. She was making sense of why teachers may make specific decisions and how those decisions fit in with the child's larger school experience.

As pre-service teachers entered their 2nd/3rd grade module, they began to ask and answer their own field notebook questions relative to individual classroom experiences. For example, in her first written reflection, one pre-service teacher asked herself: "How important is recess to children and what does it do for them physically and socially?" and "How do the administrators and teachers establish community in the school and classroom?" By the fourth and final module prior to student teaching, participants were designing their own comprehensive investigations in the capstone projects. For instance, two pre-service teachers collaborated to examine "self-selected social grouping patterns of children in the fourth and fifth grades." As the nature of the questions in the field notebook moved from teacher educator-directed (pre-k) to pre-service teacher designed (2nd/3rd) the sophistication of pre-service teacher insights moved from reflective observation to reflective inquiry. Through this series of scaffolded problem-based inquiries pre-service teachers naturally began to acknowledge and reflect on their own perspectives on teaching, learning and development.

Individual and Social Reflection

During the exit interview, one pre-service teacher recalled the beginning of the program and her first reflective writing opportunities (i.e., field notebook). At that point, pre-service teachers answered required and self-chosen questions. She said, "I was given the opportunity to be a reflective thinker. Since I had choices to respond to things that were important to me in my individual placement, it was natural for me to develop a reflective disposition." Describing her development as a reflective thinker in the exit interview, another pre-service teacher said, ". . . now I reflect without even trying. Right after a lesson I just think about it. . . . You learn a lot from yourself." These pre-service teachers indicated that reflection was encouraged at first and, over time, became a habit.

The subject of social reflection also surfaced many times in the exit interviews. Several pre-service teachers commented on the role of social reflection in their development as teacher-researchers. One pre-service teacher said, "[The projects] we did together were very helpful. We grew accustomed to planning for children together (peer to peer) which made planning with our cooperating teachers much more comfortable." Another pre-service teacher mentioned that "Discussing with peers and receiving feedback about the best way to handle specific situations has helped me better teach my students." When reflecting on her IEP project another participant said, "I felt it was important to talk to other professionals that came in contact with the child." And during the capstone project, two participants who collaborated talked often about "how to develop our results and interpret the findings." These statements corroborate that reflective dialogue between pre-service teacher peers and pre-service teachers and teaching professionals was integral to their comfort level, confidence and knowledge base.

Research Dispositions

During their capstone project, pre-service teachers talked specifically about the process through which they emerged as pre-service teacher-researchers. In the following quotes, the pre-service teacher discretely stated the many steps that she could see when looking back on the process "with fresh eyes:" "We began with the focal study and unbiased observations, and as we moved on to the IEP, we continued the skill of critically, objectively observing but we took it a step further. . . . We looked at the data collected, analyzed it and implemented an intervention. Now for our capstone project we are really drawing conclusions from our data and being able to make changes in our classroom; being able to modify instruction for individuals based on data that we've collected." Through this continuum of projects participants in the DCM were able to see the relevance of their researcher actions to the classroom setting.

RESEARCH QUESTION 2: HOW DO PRE-SERVICE TEACHER-RESEARCHERS WHO HAVE PARTICIPATED IN THE DCM MEET THE NEEDS OF INDIVIDUAL CHILDREN?

The following examples document the experiences of three pre-service teachers who are using their research skills to improve learning for the youngsters in their field settings. The first illustrates how observational data facilitated individualized literacy instruction for a low progress pupil, the second shows how reflection about a pedagogical choice empowered children in a mathematics lesson, and the third demonstrates how inquiry-based problem solving promoted equity in evaluation procedures.

Data-Based Interventions Promote Individualized Instruction

During the 2nd/3rd grade module, pre-service teachers developed Individual Education Plans, and these studies built upon skills and insights gleaned from the focal child study and the developmental study in particular. Talking about the variety of literacy levels she had observed in her 2nd grade, one pre-service teacher noticed diversity in the children's writing:

> I have . . . early writers and fluent writers, but from what I have seen, I believe that only one of my students is in the emergent writer stage. . . . After working with this child one on one, I have noticed that he cannot do the work that the other children are doing because the workbook requires reading and writing abilities. Unfortunately, this boy cannot read. . . . I noticed that he can draw beautifully, but he does not know his sounds. He can write his name as well as print very well, yet he cannot begin to form words by using letters.

After identifying this child's strengths and needs relative to literacy development, the pre-service teacher developed intervention strategies:

> I recommend taking the time to work with this child on the fundamentals of writing (instead of handing him a workbook and assigning a page number). Then, he might be able to connect letters with sounds and eventually develop his writing abilities. . . . He can overcome his difficulties with the help of others. Specifically, she states, "[Those working with this child] need to work with this child individually and not negatively focus on the fact that he is in second grade and cannot write. They should also consider using the child's drawing (artwork) as a bridge to writing. In addition, he needs to be paired up with buddies who will help him daily with his reading and writing.

The pre-service teacher used observation and other forms of data collection to document the child's strengths and needs. She interpreted the evidence and then made recommendations to those continuing to work with this boy. In doing so she clearly defined an intervention that would . . . "take the child from where he is right now and build upon his current knowledge so that he will eventually be able to read and write."

Pedagogical Choices Empower Children

This example illustrates how a pre-service teacher working on the children problem solving study was able to plan and implement an open-ended problem solving activity and use data that described each child's individual thinking strategies. The pre-service teacher predicted that the children would use three strategies: guess and test, conduct an investigation, and design a model. The following is what she discovered upon reflecting on her videotape of the lesson:

> I thought Julia would take the role of leader and guide the other students right through the problem solving experience. I was wrong. Instead, each child developed her own method. Julia's strategy was to guess and test and try different combinations of numbers. Missy tried to reduce the problem to a simpler case and she also introduced the use of a graphic organizer in the form of a table. Kendra attempted the guess and test strategy while Cassie designed a model of her own to represent the problem.

As the pre-service teacher thought about what she had just witnessed, she realized that her prediction was incorrect and recognized the impact of her child-centered delivery of the lesson on the learning outcomes: "These students were allowed to choose how they wanted to solve this problem and what materials they wanted to use to solve it. I feel that their ability to make their own choices helped to maintain their interest and momentum throughout the experience." This pre-service teacher realized that her pedagogical choice resulted in increased motivation. Each child had the freedom to follow her own inclination to test one or more possible strategies.

Testing Personal Beliefs about Best Practices for Children

The capstone project required pre-service teachers to explore teaching and learning by brainstorming personally meaningful problems and then designing a research question that would challenge them to find a practical solution. This example reflects the culminating experiences of one pre-service teacher. In previous field placements she observed assessment and evaluation practices that seemed to reflect inaccurately a given child's learning potential and understanding. She asked, "How do you approach grading to ensure that individual student understanding is reflected by the grade given?" She then explained, . . . "My research inquiry is important to what teaching and learning look like in my classroom because grades hold so much weight in our schools today. I want to make sure that I formulate a grading system that fairly and accurately reflects the individual learning needs and abilities of my students." Typical of development at each point in the scaffolded research projects, pre-service teachers in these examples were able to establish a meaningful inquiry and articulate their conclusions.

Conclusions

The purpose of this study was to describe (a) the scaffolded research experiences of individual pre-service teachers in the DCM and (b) how through scaffolded research experiences they developed a disposition for meeting the needs of individual children.

Doing research is not in itself a noble goal, but rather it is the means through which the essential tools of knowing about teaching are developed. We believe that in order for teachers to be in the habit of solving problems at the in-service level it is essential to create a milieu of inquiry at the pre-service level. Situating research at purposeful points in the program invited teachers to move beyond the role of knowledge-consumer to that of knowledge-generator (Cochran-Smith & Lytle, 1993). Our pre-service teachers progressively assumed greater responsibility for investigating their own questions about learning and teaching and became increasingly adept at accommodating children's learning needs. Multiple opportunities to review and confront their observations and hunches through dialogue with peers, cooperating teachers, and professors, helped them become more comfortable collaborating to solve the problem of how individuals learn best.

Typically, undergraduates do not do research. By the end of the DCM, however, pre-service teachers understood the value of inviting reflective, problem-based inquiry into their daily routine. They are honing the practice of inquiry, skills specific to research in the classroom and attitudes that reflect their knowledge of children as unique learners. Our hope is that teachers who graduate from the DCM will more naturally use these habits when distracted by the external demands of everyday teaching. As this research suggests, teachers who continuously research their practice are equipped to determine the impact their teaching has on student learning.

REFERENCES

Bruner, J. (1985). Vygotsky: A Historical and Conceptual Perspective. In J. Wertsch (Ed.), *Culture, Communication, and Cognition: Vygotskian Perspectives* (pp. 21–34). New York: Cambridge University Press.

Cochran-Smith, M., & Lytle, S. L. (1993). *Inside/Outside: Teacher Research and Knowledge.* New York: Teachers College Press.

Cochran-Smith, M., & Lytle, S. L. (1999). The Teacher Research Movement: A Decade Later. *Educational Researcher, 28*(7), 15–25.

Collier, S. T. (1999). Characteristics of Reflective Thought During the Student Teaching Experience. *Journal of Teacher Education, 50*(3), 173–181.

Collier, S. T. (1997, November). *Theories of Learning: Reflective Thought in Teacher Education.* Paper presented at the annual meeting of the Mid-South Educational Research Association, Memphis, TN.

Dana, N. F. & Silva, D. Y. (2001). Student Teachers as Researchers: Developing an Inquiry Stance Towards Teaching. In J. Rainer & E. Guyton (Eds.), *Research on the Effects of Teacher Education on Teacher Performance: Teacher Education Yearbook IX* (pp. 91–104). Dubuque, Iowa: Kendall/Hunt Publishing Company.

Darling-Hammond, L. & Snyder, J. (2000). Greater Expectations for Student Learning: The Missing Connections. *Liberal Education, 86*(2), 6–13.

Dewey, J. (1933). *How We Think: A Restatement of the Relation of Reflective Thinking to the Education Process.* Chicago: D. C. Health.

LaBoskey, V. K. (2001). Supporting Beginning Teacher Development through Action Research. In J. Rainer & E. Guyton (Eds.), *Research on the Effects of Teacher Education on Teacher Performance: Teacher Education Yearbook IX (pp. 195–207).* Dubuque, Iowa: Kendall/Hunt Publishing Company.

Lincoln, Y. S., & Guba, E. G. (1985). *Naturalistic Inquiry.* Thousand Oaks, CA: Sage.

Meyers, B. & Collier, S. (2000). The Developmental Cohort Model: An Innovative Pre-Service Teacher Education Program. *Journal of Professional Studies, 8*(1), 60–66.

National Center for Education Statistics (2000). *NAEP 1999 Long-Term Trends.* Washington, D.C: U.S. Department of Education.

Noddings, N. (1995). *Philosophy of Education.* Boulder, CO: Westview Press.

Pettig, K. L. (2000). On the Road to Differentiated Practice. *Educational Leadership, 58*(1), 14–18.

Price, J. N. (2001). Action Research as Transformative Practice in Pre-Service Teacher Education. In J. Rainer & E. Guyton (Eds.), *Research on the Effects of Teacher Education on Teacher Performance: Teacher Education Yearbook IX* (pp. 77-89). Dubuque, Iowa: Kendall/Hunt Publishing Company.

Sacks, S.R. & Harrington, C.N. (1982, March). *Student to Teacher: The Process of Role Transition.* Paper presented at the meeting of the American Educational Research Association, New York.

Schensul, J. J., & LeCompte, M.D. (Eds.). (1999). *Ethnographer's Tool Kit.* Walnut Creek, CA: Altamira Press.

Strauss, A. L., & Corbin, J. (1990). *Basics of Qualitative Research: Grounded Theory Procedures and Techniques.* Newbury Park, CA: Sage.

Tomlinson, C. (2000). Reconcilable Differences: Standards-Based Teaching and Differentiation. *Educational Leadership, 58*(1), 6–11.

Van den Berg, R., Sleegers, P, & Geijsel, F. (2001). Teachers' Concerns about Adaptive Teaching: Evaluation of a Support Program. *Journal of Curriculum and Supervision, 16*(3), 245–258.

Vygotsky, L. S. (1978). *Mind in Society: The Development of Higher Psychological Processes.* Cambridge, MA: Harvard University Press.

Summary and Implications

Joyce Lynn Garrett

T he three chapters in this division make it clear that working with all
children in school settings is not easy. The authors demonstrate the
ways in which many teacher education candidates come to their professional preparation programs unable to make connections between their
experiences and the work they do; remain narrowly focused and are unable
to help students generalize their experiences across time and across settings;
are not able to integrate their K–12 students' experiences into their lessons or
curriculum planning; and focus on individual action rather than on the collective, political nature of multicultural education and the education of students with disabilities. Each of these chapters exposes the discomfort all of
us feel at our initial interactions with those who are different from ourselves.
Each chapter also describes the changes that happen when students listen to
the cultural experiences of others and get involved in professional preparation that includes mentoring, reflective practice, and problem-based inquiry
as the means of heightening an individual teacher candidate's awareness. As
I read the accounts of these authors, I am reminded of the experiences
reported by teachers and students who participated in the social studies curriculum, Man A Course of Study (MACOS), developed in the late 1960's
(Educational Development Corporation, 1970).

MACOS is a yearlong curriculum designed to help participants answer
the question, "What makes man human?" Some of the major themes
addressed in the program include life cycle, structure and function, technology, communication, social organization, and culture. It is the cultural content upon which I would like to focus for the purpose of this discussion. I am
struck by the possibilities if all of us could be exposed, early in our lives as
was intended by the MACOS creators, to the kind of curriculum which presents difficult concepts utilizing the very pedagogy suggested by these
authors but including also simulations, role-playing, comparative study, and
scientific observation. I wonder how much further we might be in understanding individual and group differences if we had participated in such a
program. So, why didn't we?

It is important to note that MACOS was one of the most criticized curricula adopted by the public schools. Although readers will find many explanations of the reasons schools gradually rejected its use, the most common reason was that it introduced a different, "primitive" culture (the Netsilik Eskimos of Pelly Bay, Canada) to students and asked them to compare their own lives to those of tribal members. Many conservative groups found such exploration threatening and feared that young students would be left questioning their own culture . . . something that was intolerable. I believe it is this continuing fear, among other things, that keeps us from universally acting upon the principle that diversity adds to the richness of our society rather than diminishes it. I think it is this fear that keeps many teacher educators and their students from examining themselves and their praxis in ways that assure all teachers can teach all children.

While the three works in this division add greatly to our knowledge about enhancing the pedagogy of our teacher preparation programs, especially as we endeavor to prepare candidates who can work with all children, they also hint at a very critical piece of the equation: the need for the adequate preparation of all teacher educators so that they are able to work with all teacher education candidates. In each chapter, the authors speak of how the use of the various pedagogies positively affected their own knowledge, skills and dispositions in working with teacher education candidates; each also mentions how the authors' own practice was changed by the pedagogical processes utilized. So, why do these writers continue to decry the general insufficiency of efforts to date? They do so, because they recognize that not enough people are involved and that the narrow definition often given to diversity still hampers the work that needs to be done.

An adage well supported by the three chapters in this division as well as by Zeichner (1993) and Tatum (1994) is that teachers cannot take their students where they themselves cannot go. It is clear from the chapters here that the exposure of individuals to diverse individuals and groups is insufficient to assure their ability to teach all of America's children and youth. Only through carefully directed activities, with ample opportunity for reflection can students grow to become the kind of educators who are capable of working with a diverse student population.

Like the workforce in our public schools, the teacher education workforce remains predominately white, middle-class. The ability of many teacher educators to provide the rich experiences described in these three chapters remains elusive. Even though there are individuals who teach university classes that have a life changing effect on a select few candidates; like K–12 students, most teacher education candidates need more time, more exposure, more varied exposure, and more direct engagement with those who are different from themselves if they are to be effective in classroom settings.

The pedagogies utilized by the authors of the preceding chapters suggest that a special set of knowledge, skills, and dispositions are required of teacher educators also. Teacher educators cannot mentor, engage students in reflective inquiry, help students make databased decisions, or drive inward exploration of self, if they cannot do it themselves. Furthermore, the work of these authors suggests that continuing experiences with the same group of teacher education candidates over one or two years contributes to everyone's greater self-awareness and growth with respect to their abilities to engage K–12 students in comprehensive multicultural education.

None of these authors suggests that a single faculty member or a single three-credit course is sufficient to accomplish the goal of bringing teacher education candidates to maturity with respect to working with all children and youth. Rather, the authors in each chapter address long-term involvement with a group of qualified faculty, where students can engage in continuous reflection, continuous inquiry, and on-going assessment of their own learning as well as that of their students. What these authors do not address, and what needs to be more fully explored, are the knowledge, skills, and dispositions of teacher educators who engage in the enterprise we call teacher education . . . both the pre-service and in-service preparation of candidates.

The key to the successful incorporation of the principles of multicultural education and the broader notion of teaching all children seems to be meaningful engagement followed by meaningful reflection and mentoring. The challenge, then, becomes how we, who are responsible for the education of teachers, can become aware enough ourselves to ensure that every teacher education candidate is adequately prepared to work with all children in the schools of America. The results reported in these chapters seem to beg the question whether the pedagogies utilized in these studies could be generalized to doctoral programs that prepare teacher educators. It seems appropriate, also, to ask whether they should be considered for use by already configured faculty in colleges, schools, and departments of education. Surely we are bound, as professionals, to demand no less of ourselves than we demand of those we prepare to enter our schools. All of us must be prepared to work effectively with an ever-increasing diverse population of students.

REFERENCES

Educational Development Corporation. (1970). *Man a Course of Study*. Washington, DC: Curriculum Development Associates.

Tatum, B.D. (1994). Teaching White Students about Racism: The Search for White Allies and the Restoration of Hope. *Teachers College Record, 95,* 462–476.

Zeichner, K. M. (1993). *Educating Teachers for Cultural Diversity.* East Lansing, MI: Michigan State University.

Division

2

Preparing Educators
for Work in Urban
Schools

Overview and Framework

Charles Watson and Emma M. Savage-Davis

Charles Watson has been involved in teaching, education and school improvement for over 30 years. He has been a middle school math and science teacher, an administrator, and is currently an Associate Professor of Education at James Madison University and Director of the JMU School of Education. His research interests and his teaching are in the areas of science education and methods, school change, and teacher leadership.

Emma M. Savage-Davis is an Assistant Professor and Undergraduate Coordinator of the Middle Education Program at James Madison University. Her research interests includes teacher development, teaching in a diverse and urban society, using technology to enhance content area instruction and comprehension and the incorporation of adolescent literature as a means to discuss issues of diversity.

Overview and Framework

For over forty years, this country has lamented loudly the conditions of public, urban schools, and yet the issue has been prevalent since the turn of the 20th century. Often, the lamentations have been parallel with many of the civil rights actions, and the calls for helping the "culturally deprived child" (Riessman, 1962) were widespread. Early educational researchers began examining how universities, schools, teachers, students, and communities could help improve school achievement of the nation's poor, minority students in the cities (Weiner, 1993) and this research continues today. Some researchers and writers have suggested that schools need to adapt and change to respond to the students' different cultures (Riessman, 1962) and many others suggested alternative solutions ranging from addressing language deficiencies and differences to building on cultural strengths (Weiner, 1993). But overall, the approaches and suggestions tended to be primarily deficit models; that is, students from urban, poor, and minority cultures suffered from deficits in intelligence, opportunities, economic support, good teachers, effective bureaucracies, educational environments (including the school buildings), and other educational or cultural circumstances associated with middle-class (mostly white) suburban schools and schooling (Parker, 1968; O'Brian, 1969).

This deficit perspective appears to have continued with many of the efforts of current reformers and researchers, and although a few have proposed contextual and environmental approaches that consider the urban contexts and cultures, the model most prevalent is one that seeks to remediate and address insufficiencies and shortfalls. Perhaps the most notable exceptions to this approach are the models suggested by Martin Haberman (1988) and Daniel Liston and Kenneth Zeichner (1990). Haberman's model emphasizes specific teaching skills and techniques needed within the context of urban schools and places the needs of students as primary in the scheme of teaching behaviors. On the other hand, Liston and Zeichner underscore the moral aspects of teaching and blur the lines between teaching skills and the need for teacher activism in the social and political settings of the urban school.

In this new century, one unaltered fact remains: there is no doubt that teaching in urban schools remains daunting, even for those who are well prepared, experienced, and committed. From 30 to 60 per cent of urban students live with caregivers other than their biological parents (Hampton, Rak, & Mumford, 1997; Schwartz, 1999). Urban schools, responding to increased immigration, are becoming more crowded than their suburban counterparts (Brunett, 1995). Central city schools experience much larger and more significant shortages of teachers than suburban and rural districts (Council of Great City Schools, 1987). Urban schools often have higher teacher absenteeism, higher teacher turnover, and a greater percentage of substitute teachers (Bruno & Negrete, 1983). In 1998, more than one-third of all new teachers were hired into low-wealth and rural school districts (Recruiting New Teachers, 1999). Well organized teacher induction programs are relatively rare and teachers in urban schools have fewer opportunities for professional development and little support from colleagues (Darling-Hammond, & Sclan, 1996). Class sizes are likely to be large and teachers work under more burdensome bureaucratic limitations than teachers in suburban schools (Council for Great City Schools). Finally, there are often wide disparities in salaries and benefits between urban and suburban school districts (Council for Great City Schools).

What then, must be done? More specifically, what can teacher education programs do to address the need for qualified, compassionate, understanding, skilled, knowledgeable, and committed teachers? Furthermore, how can teacher education programs have an impact on the contextual elements of urban schools? What roles should teachers play in addressing the social, economic, and cultural factors that are repeatedly blamed for many school failures? Do urban teachers need a different set of skills, dispositions, and attitudes than their peers in suburban or wealthier schools? How do teacher educators provide stability and mentoring support for those who choose to teach in urban or poor schools?

Lois Weiner (1993, 1999) uses the words "professional trauma" to describe her first few months teaching in a typical New York City comprehensive high school; however, she then goes on to describe how she thrived for the next eight years in that same school. She writes passionately about not only addressing the needs to "fix" the schools, but about the unique qualities and experiences necessary to prepare new teachers for roles in urban schools. Weiner (1999) also suggests that there are a number of "essentials"; interestingly, both of the chapters included in this section speak to many of the essentials she views as necessary for teaching in urban schools. Her work, however, is less prescriptive than descriptive of a set of attitudes, understanding, and skills she found while she worked in urban schools. Her approach and her descriptions are grounded in the need for urban teachers to embrace their work as morally founded and politically motivated, and if empowered teachers are to work toward "fixing" the schools, the political aspects of teachers' work cannot be ignored.

Other public policy groups, many who view schools and education as linked to the economic health of the nation, are growing more involved and vocal about effectiveness and achievement in urban schools. Paul Hill and Mary Beth Celio (1998), writing for the Brookings Institution, suggest that many urban schools need "fixing" and that the responsibility for these repairs rests on the shoulders of a wider array of community leaders than simply superintendents, administrators, and teachers.

Other research and rhetoric point to ecological circumstances, often readily apparent to anyone involved or invested in urban schools, as epidemic and perhaps incurable—for example, high rates of teacher turnover and burnout, young and inexperienced teachers, high rates of criminal or unacceptable behavior, extensive and rigid bureaucratic regulations and rules, inequities in funding and monetary support, and teacher isolation. In addition, educators, and specifically teacher educators, remain faced with a distinct lack of high quality research findings from which to design and create effective teacher education programs. A recent study by Suzanne Wilson, Robert Floden, and Joan Ferrini-Mundy (2001) examines teacher preparation research and suggests that this field of research suffers from a lack of rigorous empirical studies; of over three hundred studies and articles originally included in their examination, only 57 were found to have the rigor required for their review. This is not to suggest, however, that qualitative research or for that matter, essays and opinions, are not valuable sources for insight, ideas, and results. In addition, there is much agreement that teaching in urban or schools with high rates of poverty requires either a completely different set of skills, dispositions, and understandings or different levels of skills than are generally recognized as needed for non-urban schools. Therefore, it is clear that we need to know more—more about preparing all teachers, of course, but also more about preparing teachers for urban schools.

It appears equally clear that the problems often inherent in urban schools are not solely the responsibility of teachers, nor of teacher educators. Larry Cuban (2001) warns both educators and policy-makers, however, to beware of systemic reforms that ignore the unique nature of urban and poor rural schools. He advises educators and policy-makers to recognize that the tasks facing urban educators are both different in type and magnitude from those often found in suburban districts and schools and that any model that attempts to standardize efforts are not only doomed but also harmful to students. This admonition should also apply to teacher education programs; just as urban school cultures, students, and circumstances differ widely, programs need to be conceived that address complex and difficult sets of situations and problems, while remaining clearly focused on worthwhile ends and goals.

The theme of the following two chapters is embedded in this problem and issue—that is, how do we, as teacher educators, create and implement programmatic responses to these complex and difficult issues? In the first chapter, the author reviews and synthesizes some of the prevalent research regarding educating children living in poverty and proposes five areas that emerge from the reviews as critical to educating new teachers for high poverty schools. The second chapter describes a program created and implemented in southern California that is attempting to incorporate a number of research-driven principles into an alternative licensure program for teachers in urban schools. This effort, the Accelerated Teacher Preparations Program (ACT) addresses a number of relevant and important aspects of preparing teachers for what has been earlier described as daunting.

Collaboration among university faculty and administrators, public school teachers and administrators, and other school personnel appears to be the glue that holds this successful program together, and the structure of how this program operates is perhaps unique in its approach. Furthermore, this program appears to be congruent with two important characteristics of the emerging research (Wilson, Floden, and Ferrini-Mundy, 2001) regarding the efficacy of alternative routes to licensure: alternative routes appear to attract a more diverse pool of candidates, and there appears to be more alternatively certified teachers teaching in urban settings. One other finding, that alternative routes to licensure are labor and resource-intensive, is also supported. The program makes a strong case for the institutionalization of the model for university teacher education programs, and this particular program is not experiencing a high rate of turnover or dropout.

Both chapters are noteworthy. They present both a platform for thinking about ways to address urban school needs and an interesting and effective model for reaching some of the goals for urban educators.

REFERENCES

Bruno, J. E., & Negrete, E. (1983). Analysis of Wage Incentive Programs for Promoting Staff Stability in a Large Urban School District. *The Urban Review, 15*(3), pp. 139–149.

Council of Great City Schools. (1987). *Results in the Making.* Washington DC: Author.

Cuban, L. (2001). How Systemic Reforms Harms Urban Schools. *Education Week, 20*(38), pp. 34, 35, 48.

Darling-Hammond, L., & Sclan, E. M. (1996). Who Teaches and Why: Dilemmas of Building a Profession for Twenty-First Century Schools. In J. Sikula, T. J. Buttery, E. Guyton (Eds.), *Handbook of Research on Teacher Education,* New York: Macmillan.

Haberman, M. (1988). *Preparing Teachers for Urban Schools.* Bloomington, IN: Phi Delta Kappa Educational Foundation.

Hampton, F. M., Rak, C., & Mumford, D. A. (1997). Children's Literature Reflecting Diverse Family Structures: Social and Academic Benefits for Early Reading Programs. *ERS Spectrum, 15*(4), pp. 10–15.

Hill, P. T., & Celio, M. B. (1998). *Fixing Urban Schools.* Washington DC: Brookings Institution Press.

Liston, D., & Zeichner, K. M. (1990, April). *Teacher Education and the Social Context of Schooling.* Paper presented at the annual meeting of the American Educational Research Association, Boston, MA.

O'Brian, J. L. (1969). A Master's Degree Program for the Preparation of Teachers of Disadvantaged Youth. In Tuchman, B. W., & O'Brian, J. L. (Eds.), *Preparing to teach the disadvantaged* (pp. 172–173). New York: Free Press.

Parker, J. (1968). *Staffing Schools for the Urban Disadvantaged.* Unpublished doctoral dissertation, Harvard Graduate School of Education.

Recruiting New Teacher, Inc. (1999). *Learning the Ropes: Urban Teacher Induction Programs and Practices in the United States.* Belmont MA: Author.

Riessman, F. (1962). *The Culturally Deprived Child.* New York: Harper and Row.

Schwartz, W. (1999). Family diversity in urban schools. *ERIC Clearinghouse on Urban Education* (ERIC Document Reproduction Service No. ED 434 188).

Weiner, L. (1993). *Preparing Teachers for Urban Schools.* New York: Teachers College Press.

Weiner, L. (1999). *Urban Teaching: The Essentials.* New York: Teachers College Press.

Wilson, S. M., Flooden, R. E., & Ferrini-Mundy, J. (2001). *Teacher Preparation Research: Current Knowledge, Gaps, and Recommendations.* Seattle, WA: Center for the Study of Teaching and Policy.

Educating Teachers Who Can Meet the Needs of Children Who Live in Poverty

4.

Nora Alder

Nora Alder is an Associate Professor in the School of Education at Virginia Commonwealth University. Her research interests include urban education, classroom management, and curriculum.

ABSTRACT

This chapter explores essential facets of educating teachers for work in high poverty schools including expanding experiences in poor communities, engaging in reflection, increasing historical and sociopolitical perspectives, learning about successful models of urban school reform, and informing curriculum and instructional practice.

It has long been established that children who live in poverty are more likely to drop out of school, earn less money in the workforce, be unemployed more often, and collectively cost taxpayers billions of dollars in lost earnings and taxes over time (Carnegie Council on Adolescent Development, 1989). Children of poverty are also more likely to lag behind in reading proficiency, often affecting academic performance across the board. California uses fourth grade reading scores to assess how many prisons they will need to build (Cushman, 1998). The significance of helping teachers develop practices that will change these statistics cannot be overstated. Though there is no single magic fix, evidence exists that successful, supportive, and effective classrooms that serve children who live in poverty are possible and do exist. Exploring how to better serve these students and the teachers who work with them is becoming increasingly urgent.

Five primary areas emerge from the literature as essential facets of educating teachers for having a positive impact on their work in high poverty schools: expanding pre-teachers' experiences in poor communities; engaging in self-awareness and reflection; developing an awareness of historical, socioeconomic, cultural and political factors that have influenced poverty situations; preparing teachers as active decision makers in praxis, practice, and responsiveness; and an awareness of commonalities of successful models of educational restructuring in high poverty schools. The following sections expand on these themes.

Ensuring Experience in High Poverty Communities

Based on recommendations about the need to broaden pre-service teachers' experiences in high poverty contexts, a service learning component with an emphasis on reflection is vital (Powell, Zehm & Garcia, 1996; Zeichner & Liston, 1996). Pre-service teachers need to be exposed to cultures, life styles, value systems, and material realities different from their own. Active participation in poverty environments supports intellectual understanding, communication and problem solving. Service learning and pre-student teaching practica are vital because they allow students to make direct connections between the theory and research read and discussed in classes and their first-hand experiences in the schools. In the ideal, service learning values the notion that we serve because we are in a community, not because we think other community members cannot do it themselves. A wide range of possibilities needs to be developed to ensure exposure to broader experiences than pre-service teachers bring with them. Morton (1995) points out that different understandings of service and citizenship can guide the practice of service learning, one of which is participatory democracy.

This attitude could be extended in course readings to help students understand how the "deficit model" in education effectively blames the victim (Oakes & Lipton, 1999). As students begin to work in various poverty contexts, they reflect upon what stereotypes and patterns they notice and what power relationships are evident. As importantly, students can be encouraged to identify some of the assets of their service learning communities. In this way service learning seeks to avoid the pitfalls of a kind of missionary effect that sees those we serve as deficient, or in any way less than we see ourselves.

The first and very important step in developing any service learning project consists of an investigation of site possibilities. Contact people at the site, such as school principals or assistant principals, orient the university students to the site and the kinds of work to be done there. Contact persons are also crucial in that they provide on-going support of the service learning student throughout the semester and serve as facilitator in case of conflict.

Debriefing sessions are vital as it is widely recognized that reflection enhances the understanding of experiences at the site and aids the students in making connections between those experiences and the theory discussed in classes. Reflections also help students share their experiences from the sites, understand the larger context for what they are experiencing, and dispel stereotypes.

Tutoring, mentoring and counseling in schools are useful service learning activities, especially for pre-service teachers. Habitat for Humanity, homeless organizations, the libraries, FEMA, childcare centers, child health care organizations and the local YMCA/YWCA also provide opportunities for students to develop successful service learning projects in poor communities.

Reflection

Being reflective about teaching is a worthy goal in and of itself. It is not unusual for thinking critically about teaching to help us become more articulate about, and perhaps aware of, how our philosophical underpinnings affect ways we address curricula, relate to students, and place value on social justice (Zeichner & Liston, 1996). The service learning experiences require reflective efforts from the students, as well as communication with knowledgeable professors who can help them constructively frame their experiences.

Pre-service teachers may be asked to reflect upon their own schooling experiences and to explore their personal attitudes and values about diversity, poverty, and schooling. Students need to begin to see themselves as multidimensional beings in a broad multicultural context. These discussions and their personal reactions to readings help them explore the values, assumptions and beliefs people tend to use to frame assessments of the world around them and in that way sensitize one another to the notions of multiple perspectives.

Regardless of a teachers' ethnicity, most teachers consider themselves to be middle class and could find themselves out of step with their school constituents (Alder, 2000). One of the first steps in learning to respect other points of view and how class, ethnicity and other cultural elements contribute to our development is to be aware of ourselves as cultural beings (Banks, 1996). Role playing situations involving parents, students, teachers and administrators can bring home some common issues of high poverty schools while supporting the practice of learning to value another's perspective.

Socioeconomic, Political, Historical and Political Overview

Another guiding principle for teacher educators is the acknowledged need to expand the pre-service teachers' knowledge base about the historical and policy factors that have contributed to high poverty schools in urban and rural districts in particular (Anyon, 1997; Kozal, 1991; Wilson, 1987). Anyon traces the history of Newark, New Jersey and through this case analysis builds a rationale for viewing urban education as a community problem, rapt in social and economic isolation issues, more than simply an education problem. In other words, systemic educational reform is not enough; cities themselves must be reformed. One's own contexts, the areas in which teachers are most likely to practice, are apt to provide rich background for what is outlined here.

The stratification of race, class and gender continue to be played out in urban schools. Kozol's (1991) *Savage Inequalities* and Anyon's (1997) *Ghetto Schooling: A Political Economy of Urban Educational Reform* articulate eloquently the persistence of large-scale education woes and their origins in political and economic decisions over time. The essential historical concepts in looking at schooling should include the elitist nature of early American education practice, wherein white males were more likely to be allowed to attend school, especially beyond the first three years (Oakes & Lipton, 1999).

School funding inequities that have resulted from the economic disinvestment in America's cities are well-documented (Anyon, 1997; Kozol, 1991; Wilson, 1987). Students need to be aware of these imbalances in order to understand how some schools have fallen behind in teacher salaries, physical plant maintenance, resource materials and technology. Newark (Anyon) served as a perfect prototype for what has occurred in many American cities in terms of a weakened tax base as businesses suburbanized and white flight ensued after school desegregation efforts. Anyon strongly suggests that the problems faced in Newark had beginnings that long predated the current African American control of the school district.

Teachers also need to have an understanding of the history of school segregation, desegregation and re-segregation. That schools throughout the country are as segregated today as they were in the early 1970's is well documented and a testament to failed desegregation policies and the ghettoization of African Americans and other minority groups (Oakes & Lipton, 1999). Students of urban education may find it useful to understand some of the Supreme Court and other policy decisions that have led to and maintain this reality. Further, a discussion about what many more schools and districts could have done to enable the successful implementation of court ordered desegregation of schools following the 1954 Brown v Board of Education case will help students reflect on ways their decisions and efforts impact larger effects.

The discrepancies afforded by tracking and the concomitant overrepresentation of minority students in lower, special education and vocational tracks is another concept that teachers need to explore. Resistance to the abolishment of tracking practices often comes from the section of the school community involved in the top ranked track, so interesting questions arise regarding who benefits from the current system (Stockard & Mayberry, 1992). At the same time, for all students to receive an equitable education does not mean that they all receive the same education; it means that they are all taught in ways that promote their individual opportunities to learn (Alder, 2000). Reliable placement services for students who need special educational settings necessitates a fuller understanding of the roll of culture on such things as language acquisition skills (Delpit, 1995), involvement with families, culturally and linguistically relevant curriculums, and building on student's' strengths (Warger & Burnette, 2000).

Teacher Praxis

Cooperative learning, attention to diverse learning styles, expectation effects and relevancy emerge

from the literature as prerequisite to the effective teaching of children in poverty situations (Alder, 2000). These specific aspects of teaching for meaning have been shown to boost student achievement in high poverty schools. The importance of making learning relevant to the learner, realistic expectations, the provision of specific feedback, clear communication and positive interactions between students and teachers are also vital when teaching children living in poverty (Alder). Strategies that enhance teachers' repertoire for decision making at the classroom level, including reflection, pedagogy, and successful components of models of reform are clearly vital to impact positive changes in high poverty schools (Haberman, 1991; Knapp, Addelman, Marder, McCollum, Needles, Padilla, Shields, Turnbull, & Zucker, 1995; Ladson-Billings, 1994; Rossi & Stringfield, 1997; Stockard & Mayberry, 1992; Zeichner & Liston, 1996). Successful teachers in poverty schools persistently and genuinely respect their students, involve their students in academic thought, create sustained leaning environments and are not afraid to admit their mistakes (Haberman, 1995).

New teachers need discussions about critical pedagogy, preparing students for participation in a democracy, and the importance of finding ways to empower students and help them take responsibility for their own learning. Student empowerment can range from involving students in classroom rule establishment, to presenting menus of curriculum choices, to project work that eventually produces actual experience that influence school, community, or governmental policy in the tradition of social reconstructionism (Haberman, 1991). Teachers who recoil at the notion of student empowerment have been known to rethink their positions when they are asked whether they would want their own children to feel comfortable talking in front of a city council meeting. Any skills intended to help their students make reflective decisions as related to their personal, social, and civic worlds can be construed as enhancing student empowerment. Such skills may include conflict resolution, decision making, leadership, values clarification, consensus building, or a full social reconstruction curriculum.

The appropriate uses of teaching for meaning, culturally relevant teaching, learning strategies, and discrete skill-oriented instruction are basic to all teacher education programs, but essential when teachers work with children of poverty (Alder, 2000; Haberman, 1991). The Knapp et al., (1995) study of elementary classrooms in high poverty areas clarifies teaching for meaning through rich description of student and teacher interactions in classrooms and indicates that teachers who emphasize teaching for meaning pose rigorous cognitive demands on their students early on.

Unlike the pedagogy of poverty (Haberman, 1991), wherein basic skills are the primary content of instruction in and of themselves, teaching for meaning integrates discrete skills in the context of their use and academic learning is explicitly tied to youngsters' experience. As Haberman (1991) points out, good teaching is evident when students are actively involved in issues that they consider as vital, helped in seeing the larger pictures in what they are learning, expected to question common assumptions, and asked to reflect on their own lives. Engagement is enhanced through meaningful learning objectives and experiences that demand critical thinking.

Teachers being unaware of or threatened by students' out-of-school lives hinders helping students create cognitive bridges between the knowledge they bring to school and academic knowledge (Alder, 2000). To demonstrate the knowledge and strategies needed to integrate content about various ethnic and economic groups into the mainstream curriculum is one level of making learning relevant. A deeper level calls for a determination to know students individually and in and out of the classroom context. Ladson-Billings (1994) discuss relevance as not only a motivational theory that helps students see the rationale for their studies, but as the way teachers tie content to their real life experiences. One of Ladson-Billings' expert teachers, for example, helps students recognize the similarities between the constitutions that underpin their churches with the constitution that serves our country. Books with protagonists students can relate to in terms of ethnicity are sought out by teachers in her study and included in the curricula. Knapp et al. (1995) also present explicit examples of teacher behaviors that are actively and constructively responsive to student diversity. Underscoring the importance of holding high expectations for students in academics and behavior, actively constructive teachers make it a point to include those cultures' major accomplishments in the curriculum.

A full discussion of learning styles should not be limited to visual, auditory and kinesthetic strengths and weaknesses, though these are clearly a part of such discourse. Some of the similarities and differences in learning styles theories such as global versus analytical, field dependent versus field independent, or right brain versus left brain help teachers see that differences are, in fact, important considerations in our work with students. Unless we help teachers understand how to use this information to explicitly enrich their work with students, teachers are apt to teach to their personal learning style strength. Knapp et al., (1995) found that actively constructive teachers paid attention to building on the strengths and building up the weaknesses of the learning styles of their children in high poverty schools. Because learning styles are sometimes tied to culture, one teacher, for example, accommodates her Asian students by making certain some assignments allow for self-direction and independence, while others require interaction with their peers.

Learning styles may be best served by tying them to the basic motivational technique of variety. Cooperative learning groups, dyads, simulations, direct instruction and individual seatwork all have their places in the high poverty classroom (Alder, 2000). Teachers need to develop libraries of optional exercises for students who finish work earlier than others, or who are interested in knowing more about subjects at hand. Meanwhile, other students need this time to think out their responses to tasks. As we have known for some time (Dewey, 1934), some students learn well through reading, while others need more active experiences. Generally, it is a good idea to set the stage for each concept with a big picture and then follow up with more in-depth instruction. Presentations need to be at once systematic and personal, blending meaning and value with logic. Further, students need to be asked to engage in a variety of convergent and divergent thinking.

Finally, provide students with multiple ways of learning and multiple ways of demonstrating what they have learned.

On a continuum from disorderly to orderly, Knapp et al. (1995) note that even orderly classrooms vary in type from restrictive to enabling. Enabling classrooms are more consistent, evidence thoughtful prevention, and enable enthusiastic learning. Though teachers who manage enabling and orderly classes employ measures such as "time-outs", students are soon welcomed back into the group as a whole. In this way these teachers underscore their care for individual students and their value of the group as a whole (Noddings, 1992). Personal relationships with students, rich in acceptance and care, are a trademark of teachers who run orderly and enabling classrooms.

Models of Reform

Popular models for restructuring have varied focus points. One focal point may be to involve teachers in action research, needs assessments and field testing of hypothetical solutions to contextual conceptions of their schools' problems. Another model may focus on reading improvement, curriculum, or classroom management improvement (Stringfield, Datnow, Ross, & Snively, 1998). Models may support notions of concentrating on the three R's and cutting out electives, or they may support electives as a way to build on student interests and strengths (Rossi & Stringfield, 1997).

Successful models tend to have several commonalities, including involving parents, empowering teachers and students and focusing on continuous progress, problem solving and teamwork. Some system to provide support for students who are academically behind is key to comprehensive school reform (Odden, 2000; Olatokunbo & Slavin, 1997; Rossi & Stringfield, 1997).

Though costly, an array of comprehensive models for restructuring schools have been instituted across the country with somewhat varied success (Odden, 2000; Rossi & Stringfield, 1997). Because successful school restructuring is possible using diverse strategies, schools need to be able to make thoughtful and well-informed choices about which model of reform is most appropriate to their context. Multidimensional support and leadership from the district site administrators and state departments of education are essential. Equally important is that the individual faculty understands and buys into the model. Finally, adaptations to school reform models are to be expected and encouraged so that they speak to the specific needs of each site.

The Professional Development School model may be one way to effectively reduce costs typically associated with school wide reform efforts. In these situations, volunteer university teacher education faculty provide staff development for public school faculty. Pre-service teachers enrolled at the university have access to more on-site experience and all partners have the opportunity to move toward more research-based reform. Partnerships (Cole & Ramey, 2000) report better preparation of pre-service teachers for their work in urban schools. Outcomes depend on the focus of the partnerships and the resources available to implement strategies, but such partnerships may increase the number of staff development workshops available in those schools, increase the numbers of tutors and mentors, and increase parental involvement.

Rossi and Stringfield (1997) report that creating a climate of schools as learning communities is strongly associated with effective school reform.

> A sense of "community" is concerned with the deep-structure fabric of interpersonal relations. Soundly woven, this fabric permits a shared frame of reference and supports mutual expectations. The relations among adults in schools provide models of behavior for students. The ways in which teachers, administrators, and classified staff persons relate to students also define the conditions within which teaching and learning of specific subject matters take place. In addition, these relations determine a school's readiness to undertake and sustain efforts to achieve shared goals (e.g., making a campus a safe haven or raising reading achievement scores), and they define a school's image in its neighborhood-for parents, other residents, local business-persons and shopkeepers, and community-based service organizations. The quality of these relations is critical to all facets of school operation, yet it is typically taken for granted. In our experience, the quality of these relations in typical schools is much lower than it must be if schools are to be productive (p. 47).

The development of a shared vision, incorporation of diversity, communication and participation, relationships built on caring, trust, teamwork, respect, and recognition among faculty and students are all necessary components of creating a sense of community in schools (Rossi & Stringfield).

Conclusion

Preparing teachers to meet the needs of high poverty students is a daunting task. Expert teachers, who understand the historical, political, social, instructional, curricular and managerial aspects of education are vital if we are to raise the standards of living for generations of youngsters and their families. Beyond the basics of reading writing and mathematics, schools need to find ways to help students become critical thinkers, fully capable of active, constructive participation in a democracy, fully aware of their responsibility for their own growth and development, and fully proficient in methods that enable intelligent social change.

REFERENCES

Alder, N. (2000). Teaching Minority Students. *Multicultural Perspectives.* 2(2), 28–31.

Anyon, J. (1997). *Ghetto Schooling: A Political Economy of Urban Educational Reform.* New York: Teachers College Press.

Banks, J. (1996). *Teaching Strategies for Ethnic Studies.* Boston: Allyn and Bacon.

Carnegie Council on Adolescent Development (1989). *Turning Points.* New York: Carnegie Corporation of New York.

Cole, D.J. and Ramey, L. (2000). *Joining Forces: A Collaborative Venture to Develop Exemplary Field Partnership School Sites* (ERIC Document Reproduction Service No. ED 438 278).

Cushman, K. (1998). Democracy and equity: CES's tenth common principle. *The Coalition of Essential Schools, 14*(3), 1–8.

Delpit, L. (1995). *Other People's Children: Cultural Conflict in the Classroom.* New York: The New Press.

Dewey, J. (1934). *Experience and Education.* New York: Collier Books.

Haberman, M. (1991). The Pedagogy of Poverty Versus Good Teaching. *Phi Delta Kappan, 73*(4), 290–294.

Haberman, M. (1995). Selecting "Star" Teachers for Children and Youth in Urban Poverty. *Phi Delta Kappan, 76*(10), 777–781.

Knapp, M. S., Addelman, N. E., Marder, C., McCollum, H., Needles, M.C., Padilla, C., Shields, P. M., Turnbull, B. J., and Zucker, A. A. (1995). *Teaching for Meaning in High Poverty Classrooms.* New York: Teachers College.

Kozol, J. (1991). *Savage Inequalities.* New York: Harper Perennial.

Ladsen-Billings, G. (1994). *The Dreamkeepers: Successful Teachers of African American Children.* San Francisco, CA: Jossey-Bass.

Liston, D. P. and Zeichner, K. M. (1996). *Culture and Teaching.* Mahwah, New Jersey: Lawrence Erlbaum Associates.

Morton, K. (1995). The Irony of Service: Charity, Project and Social Change in Service Learning. *Michigan Journal of Community Service Learning, 2,* 19–32.

Noddings, N. (1992). *The Challenge to Care in Schools: An Alternative Approach to Education.* New York, Teachers College Press.

Oakes, J. and Lipton, M. (1999). *Teaching to Change the World.* McGraw-Hill, Boston.

Olatokunbo, S.F. and Slavin, R. E. (1997). Promising Programs for Elementary and Middle Schools: Evidence of Effectiveness and Replicability. *Journal of Education for Students Placed at Risk, 2*(3), 251–307.

Odden, A. (2000). The Costs of Sustaining Educational Change through Comprehensive School Reform. *Phi Delta Kappan, 81*(6), 433–438.

Powell, R. R., Zehm, S. and Garcia, J. (1996). *Field Experience: Strategies for Exploring Diversity in Schools.* Englewood Cliffs, New Jersey: Prentice-Hall.

Rossi, R. J. and Stringfield, S. C. (1997). *Studies of Education Reform: Education Reform and Students at Risk.* Washington: Office of Educational Research and Improvement, U.S. Department of Education.

Stockard, J. and Mayberry, M. (1992). *Effective Educational Environments.* Newbury Park, California: Corwin Press.

Stringfield, S., Datnow, A., Ross, S.M., Snively, F. (1998). Scaling Up School Restructuring in Multicultural, Multilingual Contests: Early Observations from Sunland County. *Education and Urban Society, 30,* 3, 326–357.

Warger, C. and Brunette, J. (2000). *Five Strategies to Reduce Overrepresentation of Culturally and Linguistically Diverse Students in Special Education.* ERIC/OSEP Digest E596.

Wilson, W. J. (1987). *The Truly Disadvantaged: The Inner City, the Underclass, and Public Policy.* Chicago: The University of Chicago Press.

Zeichner, K.M. and Liston, D. P. (1996). *Reflective Teaching: An Introduction.* Mahwah, New Jersey: Lawrence Erlbaum Associates.

The ACT Program

5.

Redesigning Teacher Education
to Meet Urban Needs and
Teacher Shortages

Judy Lombardi, Christine Smith, Nancy Burstein, and James Cunningham

Dr. Judy Lombardi is an assistant professor of secondary education at California State University and Coordinator of the ACT Secondary Program. Her specializations include teacher preparation, methods of teaching English/ESL, and critical thinking.

Dr. Nancy Burstein is a professor of special education at California State University Northridge, DELTA Collaborative Coordinator, and Coordinator of the ACT Special Education Program. Her specializations include teacher education, urban education, and special education.

Dr. Christine Smith is professor emeritus of secondary education at California State University Northridge, DELTA Collaborative Coordinator, and Co-Director of the DELTA pre-intern/intern program. Her specializations include teacher preparation and adolescent and adult literacy.

Dr. James Cunningham is professor emeritus of secondary education at California State University Northridge and Coordinator of the ACT instructional technology component. His specialties are teacher preparation, science education, and instructional technology.

ABSTRACT

This paper discusses the key features, components, and outcomes of the Accelerated Collaborative Teacher (ACT) program, a one-year full time field based program designed to address an acute teacher shortage of teachers in urban schools. We describe efforts to enhance the recruitment, preparation, and retention of teachers through a school-university partnership and an emphasis on preparing teachers to serve diverse urban learners. Evaluation findings indicate that ACT attracts a diverse population with the majority of participants successful in completing the program in one year. Graduating ACT students report that they are prepared or well prepared to serve diverse urban learners and the majority of graduates teach in urban schools. Critical to the success of the ACT Program has been the restructuring of teacher education as a school-university responsibility with support provided to facilitate program coordination and collaboration.

This paper describes the principal features and outcomes of the Accelerated Teacher Preparation (ACT) Program, a one-year full time program designed to provide qualified teachers for urban schools. Supported by a five-year grant from the Weingart Foundation, ACT was developed through the Design for Excellence: Linking Teaching and Achievement (DELTA) Collaborative, an initiative of the Los Angeles Annenberg Metropolitan Project (LAAMP). The DELTA Collaborative was established to develop a model for schools and universities to work in partnership in educating aspiring, new and experienced teachers and consists of four PreK-12 school families, each linked to a state university in California. A major goal of the Collaborative is to restructure teacher education as a shared responsibility between schools and universities, with an emphasis on teacher preparation programs that are field-based and designed to prepare teachers to serve diverse, urban learners.

The Need for Qualified Teachers in Urban Schools

The crisis in urban schools is growing. While a qualified teacher is one of the most important factors in improving student achievement, few credentialed teachers are hired in urban areas (Darling-Hammond, 1996). In Los Angeles, for example, one quarter of the city's 34,000 teaching population are hired with emergency certification, with little preparation or experience in teaching and that number is growing (Center for Future Teaching and Learning, 1999). Moreover, attrition rates for new teachers in urban districts can sometimes reach 50 percent in the first five years of teaching because of inadequate preparation and the lack of high-quality mentoring and induction programs (Archer, 1999; U.S. Department of Education, 1998).

Given teacher shortages, urban school classrooms are increasingly being staffed by teachers who have little experience or preparation in teaching. In California, teachers with emergency certification are hired with only a bachelor's degree, a passing grade on a basic skills test, and 40 hours of generalized training required in the first year. According to Phyllis Gudoski, veteran teacher and PreK–12 DELTA/ACT Coordinator, "We wouldn't even hire a plumber who didn't know what to do, but we're content to have those people teach our kids with very little training? Why are we doing this to our kids? It amazes me that we don't have a public outcry" (Chiang, 1998, p. 3).

Few teacher candidates, particularly those in urban areas, are available to participate in traditional programs that require student teaching in assigned classrooms with supervising teachers. Instead, they enter alternative certification programs designed for on-the-job teachers. A 1998 survey of state departments of education reported that 41 states and the District of Columbia offer some type of alternative teacher certification. During the 1990s, more than 80,000 teachers entered the profession using alternative pathways; 24% of the 41 states and the District of Columbia report increased enrollments in alternative programs over the last five years (Hirsch, 2001). Darling-Hammond reports that 60% of alternatively trained teachers leave teaching by their third year, as compared to 30% of traditionally trained teachers and 10-15% of teachers in five-year programs (in Berry, 2000). Moreover, Berry indicates that in these truncated programs, teachers are ill-prepared to teach.

> The most compelling evidence against these short-cut programs may be reams of research studies revealing that both content and teaching knowledge matter for student achievement. Studies in these areas have shown that knowledge of subject matter and of teaching and learning acquired in teacher education are strongly correlated with teacher performance in the classroom, and that teacher education coursework is sometimes more influential than additional subject matter preparation in promoting student's mathematics and science achievement (p. 3).

While there is concern about the quality and retention of teachers participating in alternative certification programs (Darling-Hammond, 2000), significant concerns also exist regarding the preparation of teachers in conventional university programs. Common concerns reported by researchers of university-based programs include an emphasis of theory over practice, weak linkages between coursework and fieldwork, poor quality of student teaching experiences, and limited early clinical experiences

(Bullough, Hobbs, Kauchak, Crow, Stokes, 1997; Hart & Burr, 1996; Kleinasser & Paradis, 1997; Rigden, 1996). To address the concerns of both conventional and alternative preparation programs, educators emphasize that teacher preparation programs need to be redesigned as a shared responsibility of schools and universities (Fullan, 1994; Kochan & Kunkel, 1998; Metcalf-Turner & Fischetti, 1996; Sandholtz & Finan, 1998). Through these partnerships, universities and schools coordinate their efforts to simultaneously improve schools and the education of teachers (Carnegie Forum, 1986; Holmes Group, 1986; Winitzky, Stoddart, and O'Keefe, 1992).

Providing Qualified Teachers for Urban Schools

The ACT Program was established to improve the quality of teachers in urban schools by restructuring teacher education as a shared responsibility. As one of the four school families participating in the DELTA Collaborative, the Francis Polytechnic (Poly) Family of schools in the Los Angeles Unified School District (LAUSD) was paired with California State University, Northridge (CSUN). The Poly Family serves almost 18,000 students in 14 schools, 10 elementary, 2 middle, 1 high school, and 1 alternative high school. Poly schools have approximately 800 teachers, over 20% with emergency certification. Students come primarily from low-income families diverse in language and culture. CSUN is one of the largest public institutions in California graduating over 1, 000 teachers annually.

The CSUN/Poly Collaborative was interested in creating an alternative to traditional university and alternative certification programs, encompassing, as recommended by Huling, Resta, & Rainwater (2001), the strengths and minimizing the weaknesses of each of the two predominant delivery systems in teacher preparation. The ACT program's major objectives included:

- Developing recruitment strategies to attract candidates from diverse backgrounds, willing to commit a year to obtain a credential prior to employment as a teacher.
- Designing and implementing a program with shared school-university collaboration that reflected best practices in teacher preparation.
- Enhancing teacher retention through a support system for teacher candidates and professional preparation focused on serving students in urban schools.

ENHANCING TEACHER RECRUITMENT FOR URBAN SCHOOLS

Given a limited supply of teachers for urban schools, the literature suggests that proactive recruitment strategies are needed to attract a diverse teacher population. These strategies include targeting universities that serve large numbers of students of color, paraprofessionals working in urban schools, and older and often second career graduate students who comprise one in three new teachers entering the field (Genzuk, Lavadenz, & Krashen, 1994; Hardman, 1997). Recruitment is enhanced by customer-oriented programs that facilitate administrative procedures (e.g., admission and registration for courses) and provide cohort groups, readily accessible locations, and financial assistance (Huling, et al., 2001; Villegas, Clevell, Anderson, Goertz, Joy, Bruchi & Irvine, 1995).

Recruitment efforts play a crucial role in the ACT Program. A recruitment coordinator, responsible for identifying and attracting ACT applicants, widely advertises the program through flyers distributed to schools and posted at the university; information on a university Web site; personal interviews with prospective candidates; meetings with local school administrators and teachers; and newspaper announcements. Also emphasized is the program support provided through ACT including financial incentives (through grant stipends and university assistance), guaranteed course enrollment, and support services such as individualized advisement and mentoring and participation in a cohort-based program.

IMPROVING THE PREPARATION AND RETENTION OF URBAN-SCHOOL TEACHERS

The Collaborative focused on developing a program that reflected best practices in preparing and retaining teachers for urban schools. First, to facilitate school-university collaboration, cross-institutional positions were created to coordinate the DELTA Collaborative: two full-time positions shared by three university faculty members, one each from the Departments of Elementary, Secondary, and Special Education, and a full time PreK–12 Coordinator from the Poly Family. Second, Coordinators conducted an assessment with Poly personnel and parents and CSUN faculty regarding program needs in teacher preparation. Finally, Coordinators completed an extensive review of the literature on teacher preparation and multicultural and urban education to assist in program development.

Reflecting the needs assessment and research on best practices in teacher preparation, the ACT Program was designed over a two-year period and involved members of the DELTA Steering Committee, comprised of school personnel and university faculty, a task force of university faculty with school representation, and faculty writing teams who consulted with the Steering Committee (For a detailed description of the ACT Program development see Burstein, Kretschmer, Smith & Gudoski, 1999). As a result of these efforts, the program incorporated the following principles that guided program development.

A Standards-Based Curriculum

Initiatives establishing standards of teacher performance have gained momentum during the past decade (Darling-Hammond, 1996; Otis-Wilborn & Winn, 2000). California adopted the California Standards for the Teaching Profession (CSTP) (California Commission, 1997) for beginning teachers, which provided the framework for the ACT program, assisting faculty in developing a common understanding of what teachers need to know and be able to do. These standards, organized around six interrelated domains, include: engaging and supporting all students in learning; creating and maintaining effective environments for student learning; understanding and organizing subject matter for student learning; planning instruction and designing learning experiences for all students; assessing student learning; and developing as a professional educator. They form the basis for determining course content and pedagogy, assessing teacher candidates throughout their year of study, and evaluating their teaching competencies.

Developmental Approach to Teaching

Research suggests that new teachers undergo a developmental process in acquiring the knowledge, skills, and attitudes critical to their work (Kagan, 1992; Wideen, Mayer-Smith & Moon, 1998). Reflecting this developmental approach to learning, the ACT Program is conceptualized in modules rather than coursework. Each module has three interconnected components, a common core for all teacher candidates, and specialization coursework and field experiences. The modules align with the six CSTP standards and emphasize specific themes that spiral and are interwoven throughout the curriculum, reflecting a developmental approach to learning.

Emphasis on the Diverse Urban Learner

Teachers are often ill-prepared to serve students from diverse backgrounds; they are typically from different backgrounds than their students and have little knowledge about the sociocultural factors that influence minority students' performance in school (Obiakor & Schwenn, 1996; Winzer & Mazuerek, 1998).

Moreover, teachers know little about their own cultural backgrounds and how these influence their educational practices (Harry, Rueda, & Kalyanpur, 1999). Practitioners can most effectively learn to meet the needs of children and families from different backgrounds when cultural diversity is infused within the context of every course and field experience (Artiles & Trent, 1994; Burstein, Cabello & Hamann, 1993; Obiakor & Utley, 1997). Cultural competency is facilitated by providing opportunities for reflection through support groups and interactions with individuals from diverse ethnic backgrounds, and ongoing professional development to faculty, increasing their multicultural knowledge and skills (Grant, 1994; Landson-Billings, 1995; McAllister & Irvine, 2000; Voltz, Dooley & Jeffries, 1999).

The ACT Program offers a Cross-Cultural Language and Academic Development (CLAD) credential or a Bilingual CLAD credential emphasis (BCLAD) for elementary and secondary teacher candidates. Program objectives for the CLAD credential focus on three domains infused throughout the program: (a) language structure and first and second language development; (b) methodology of bilingual, English language development and content instruction; and (c) culture and cultural diversity. This content is infused throughout the curriculum. Faculty meet on an ongoing basis to discuss their own knowledge and skill in teaching about multicultural education, share with one another their expertise, discuss students' stages of development and readiness for specific concerns and multicultural activities, and provide opportunities for reflection and support among teacher candidates. Through planning and debriefing sessions, faculty report that they have grown in their knowledge and skills in preparing teachers for diverse urban learners, promoting the development of teaching practices that are culturally responsive.

Collaborative Learning and Teaching Community

School-university collaboratives create a professional learning and teaching community where educators (i.e., faculty, classroom teachers, and teacher candidates) are immersed collectively in sharing knowledge, inquiry, and problem solving (Darling-Hammond & McLaughlin, 1995; Darling-Hammond, 1996; Veal & Rickard, 1998). Learning through this process facilitates the development of reflective professionals who can respond to the complex and diverse needs of students in urban schools (Harry, Rueda, & Kalyanpur, 1999; Pleasants, Johnson & Trent, 1998; Soto & Goetz, 1998).

The ACT preparation program was structured as a collaborative learning and teaching community organized around the school, rather than the university calendar. To facilitate school-university collaboration, most courses are held at the Professional Development Center (PDC) at a high school in the Poly Family. The program was designed to recruit cohorts of students and to provide a variety of collaborative opportunities for teacher candidates to network with students, faculty, and collaborating teachers/coaches. Cadres of university faculty and classroom teachers trained as coaches share knowledge and bridge theory/practice in team teaching the three course modules. This shared knowledge promotes articulation across content areas and develops a framework of interrelated understandings among participants (Burstein et al., 1999).

Ongoing and Coordinated Field Experiences

Researchers emphasize the need for field-based programs in which teacher candidates experience a rich array of fieldwork across grade levels and intensive teaching experiences in specialization areas (Darling-Hammond & McLaughlin, 1995; Hart & Burr, 1996; Rigden, 1996; Shanker, 1996). However, field experiences are often cited as the weakest component in teacher education, with collaborating teachers and university faculty often working at cross-purposes (Winitzky et al., 1992

Field experiences are designed as an integral part of the ACT Program, increasing over time and building upon previous experiences. Teacher candidates work with students in participating schools who come primarily from low-income families diverse in language and culture. Teachers who demonstrate exemplary practices are selected as coaches and trained in the California Formative Assessment and Support System for Teachers (CFASST), a program designed to prepare professional educators to support and assess beginning teachers. Coaches in collaboration with university supervisors are responsible for supervision and evaluation. Finally, fieldwork seminars are provided in each module, assisting teacher candidates in developing teaching practices through inquiry, reflection and analysis.

A Supportive Learning Environment

Teachers, just as other learners, are more likely to complete preparation if they participate in a learning environment that provides academic and personal support (Villegas, et al., 1995). Considerable emphasis in the ACT program is on providing support and guidance to teacher candidates. ACT Coordinators are responsible for these efforts, meeting with teacher candidates initially and throughout the program to monitor their progress and assess their needs.

Advisement begins with project faculty interviewing each program applicant, addressing initial questions about admission procedures, program requirements and program support (e.g., financial aid, the Learning

Resource Center, services provided to candidates with disabilities). A program orientation is held at the beginning of each year with faculty explaining requirements and support available on and off campus and addressing questions or concerns regarding the program. The ACT Coordinators meet with teacher candidates in each module, providing information on credential requirements aside from coursework (e.g., subject matter competence exams), and informing them of examination schedules, study materials, and workshops. Throughout the year at program planning meetings, coordinators and faculty discuss student progress and provide assistance for those with academic or personal needs.

In summary, the ACT Program was designed to reflect research and effective practices in the recruitment, preparation, and retention of teachers for urban schools. Through active and comprehensive recruitment strategies that attract diverse teacher candidates, a preparation program that emphasizes competencies in serving urban students diverse in culture and language, and a comprehensive support system, it was anticipated that the ACT Program would address the need to increase the quantity and quality of educators in urban schools. Key features of the ACT Program include:

- A standards-based curriculum, reflecting the California Standards for the Teaching Profession
- Emphasis on field-based experiences with diverse learners, linking theory to effective teaching practices
- Courses collaboratively taught by a cadre of university faculty and classroom teachers
- Coursework offered both at the Poly Professional Development Center and at CSUN
- Supervision by experienced classroom teachers trained as coaches
- Personalized advisement and mentoring
- Progression through the program as a cohort

ACT Program Format

The ACT Preparation Program was designed to accelerate the credentialing process through a one-year, full-time graduate program for elementary, secondary, and special education teacher candidates. ACT consists of three modules and a total of 36–39 credit hours, beginning in June of each year and ending in June of the following year. Each module has three components: (a) a common core of courses for all students; (b) specialization courses in elementary, secondary, and special education and (c) field experiences aligned with both core and specialized curriculum (see table 1). In addition to coursework required in the ACT program, ACT candidates must meet state and university requirements. These include a passing score on the California Basic Educational Skills Test (CBEST), knowledge of the U.S. Constitution demonstrated by course or exam, verification of subject matter knowledge and writing proficiency, and a course in multicultural studies.

The Common Core

Offered during each module, the common core is a series of courses that provide a foundation of knowledge and skills in educational practices. Reflecting a developmental approach to learning, the core focuses on themes, including learning and development, exceptionality, culture and cultural diversity, and technology, that are introduced in the first module and revisited in the second and third, providing a deeper level of understanding and opportunity for reflection with candidate development of competencies.

The Core is taught collaboratively by a team of university faculty, classroom teachers, administrators, and parents. Many assignments during each module's core and specialization courses are based on the candidates' fieldwork, in which they reflect on and discuss their classroom observation and teaching experiences with faculty. Two ACT Web sites, one on the program as a whole and another encompassing common core module syllabi and assignments, help faculty and candidates stay current and informed about the program. Teacher candidates develop a portfolio of lesson plans, student samples, and other artifacts, in order to document competency in meeting the California Standards for the Teaching Profession.

Specialization Courses

Building on the Common Core, specialization courses are provided in each module in elementary, secondary, and special education. Teacher candidates from the common core attend the appropriate specialization courses, either at the Professional Development Center or on the CSUN campus where ACT participants join other teacher candidates (e.g., small enrolled courses such as math or art methods).

Fieldwork

Fieldwork is an integral part of the ACT Program. Teacher candidates complete classroom participation and observation activities in the first module,

TABLE 1
The ACT Program Modules

Program Components	ACT Candidates	Module I Summer, 8 weeks	Module II Fall, 15 weeks	Module III Spring, 23 weeks
Common Core	All ACT Candidates	Getting Started: Introduction to Teaching (4 units)	Moving Forward: Meeting Needs Of All Students (4 units)	Putting It All Together: The Reflective Practioner (4 units)
Specialization	Elementary	Foundations in Literacy in Multicultural Schools (2 units)	Literacy Instruction in Multicultural Schools (2 units) Mathematics Curriculum and Methods (2 units)	History/Social Science Curriculum and Methods (2 units)
	Secondary	Fundamentals of Teaching in Multiethnic, Multilingual Schools (4 units)	Specialized Methods (3 units) Developing as a Professional in the Secondary School (1 unit)	Teaching Reading and Writing in Multilingual Secondary Schools (4 units)
	Special Education	Foundations of Special Education (2 units) Foundations of Literacy in Multicultural Schools (2 units)	Educational Programming and Instructional Adaptations for Exceptional Learners (3 units) Literacy Instruction in Multicultural Schools (2 units)	Positive Behavioral Support (3 units) Curriculum and Instruction for Students with Mild/Moderate/ Severe Disabilities (3 units)
Fieldwork	Elementary	Introduction to Teaching Field Experience and Seminar (2 units)	Introductory Student Teaching and Seminar (4 units)	Student Teaching and Seminar (6 units)

(continued on next page)

TABLE 1 (continued)				
Program Components	ACT Candidates	Module I Summer, 8 weeks	Module II Fall, 15 weeks	Module III Spring, 23 weeks
	Secondary	Introduction to Teaching Field Experience and Seminar (2 units)	Advanced Field Experience and Seminar (4 units)	Student Teaching and Seminar (6 units)
	Special Education	Introduction to Teaching Field Experience and Seminar (2 units)	Field Experience and Seminar (4 units)	Advanced Fieldwork with Exceptional Learners and Seminar (6 units)

team-teach and do some stand-alone teaching in the second module, and assume full responsibility for the classroom in the third module. Teacher candidates are assigned to teachers selected and trained as coaches. Each field experience is linked to a seminar where teacher candidates are encouraged to draw from their field experiences as they examine theory and pedagogy, apply knowledge to their own situations, and reflect upon these experiences in portfolios and fieldwork journals.

DELTA Coordinators meet weekly for program planning and to address program concerns. Faculty members from all the involved specialization courses meet once a semester to share syllabi, share teaching strategies, and monitor overlap of concepts and activities. Each ACT Coordinator is responsible for advising students and meeting with core faculty for planning and decision-making. Through these carefully planned and collaborative efforts, the program blends a balance of theory and practice, providing intensive coursework, collaboration, and a year of fieldwork experiences at local, urban schools.

Program Evaluation and Outcomes

Program evaluation has been an integral part of the DELTA Collaborative and is conducted each year to inform program practices. Evaluation includes questionnaires and interviews, surveying ACT teacher candidates, university K–12 faculty, and the CSUN and Poly community. Three major sources of evaluation data are reported in this paper, focusing on ACT outcomes related to recruitment, preparation and retention: demographic information on teacher candidates, surveys conducted with graduating ACT teacher candidates regarding their competencies in teaching, and follow-up data on the employment of ACT graduates. The quantitative data from surveys is analyzed and qualitative data examined for common themes. Using the survey results and narrative comments, coordinators and evaluators examine trends in responses and program areas that need improvement.

RECRUITMENT

A major goal of the ACT Program is to recruit a diverse group of teacher candidates to a full-time program. Four years of recruitment data (1998–02) indicate that the number of ACT participants has grown steadily since 1999, suggesting that recruitment efforts and the growing reputation of the ACT Program are attracting teacher candidates who are willing to devote a year to pre-service education *prior* to accepting a teaching position.

As shown in Figure 2, ACT teacher candidates are from diverse backgrounds. While the majority are white (64%), 34% are from underrepresented groups, predominantly Hispanic (20%) and Asian (9%). Moreover, ACT candidates are diverse in gender (24% are male) and age (ranging from 21–65, with a mean age of 33), and include young graduating seniors and

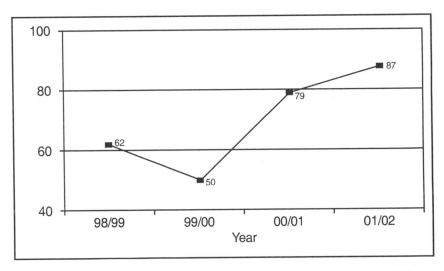

Figure 1. Number of Teacher Candidates Enrolled in ACT

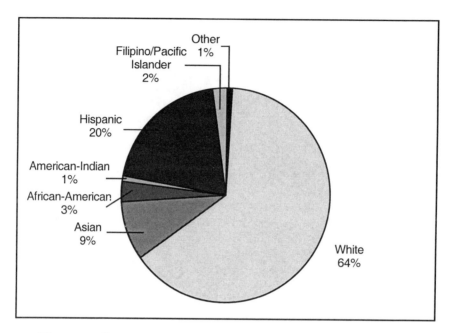

Figure 2. Ethnic Background of ACT Teacher Candidates

older individuals who are changing careers. Finally, ACT candidates are diverse in academic backgrounds. They come from numerous undergraduate majors and most meet and exceed the minimum grade point average (GPA) of 2.75. However, applicants are accepted with lower GPAs if they have strong recommendations, work experience with children and/or have passed CBEST. Participating in the program are also several candidates with learning and physical disabilities. These demographic data suggest that the ACT program attracts candidates from a wide range of backgrounds, enriching the program and contributing to the diversity of teachers in urban schools.

TEACHER PREPARATION

Evaluation on teacher preparation includes two surveys distributed to graduating ACT candidates each year, an internal evaluation developed by ACT coordinators and faculty and an external evaluation developed through the DELTA Collaborative. The internal evaluation includes items to be rated on a 5-point scale from 1, *not well prepared* to 5, *very well prepared* and includes questions on the strengths of the ACT program and areas that need improvement. As shown in Table 2 for the year 1999–2000, the average mean rating was 4.2 on a five-point scale, with ACT candidates indicating that they are *well prepared* or *very well prepared* as teachers. Representative narrative comments on the ACT Program summarize candidates' experiences in the program.

I feel more prepared going in as a teacher now than if I went in on an emergency permit. This program has taught me so much, that I will be able to take into the classroom (Elementary Education Candidate).

I feel so much more confident as a result of this program. I came in unsure of my place in the classroom and now feel competent to be in the classroom (Secondary Education Candidate).

TABLE 2
ACT Candidate Program Evaluation Summary, 1999–2000

Criteria	Rating
Meet the CSTP	4.6
Address diversity in planning and teaching	4.3
Reflect critically on their own teaching practice	4.3
Motivate all students to learn	4.2
Address exceptionality in planning and teaching	4.2
Interact with students and parents	4.2
Create effective lesson plans	4.2
Consult with other professionals for information and assistance	4.2
Incorporate best practices in teaching	4.1
Manage classroom behavior effectively	4.1
Plan collaboratively with other professionals	4.1
Mean rating =	4.2

I think I am ten times as prepared for my first year of teaching, because of the experiences and exposure to different situations, populations of students and teaching styles (Special Education Candidate).

The external evaluation is comprised of 27 items related to teacher preparation. On a five-point scale from 1, *strongly disagree* to 5, *strongly agree,* the average mean rating was 4.2. Items included overall preparation for teaching, linking theory with practice, collaboration with colleagues, serving diverse urban learners, and working with parents. Taken together, these data indicate that teacher candidates value their preparation through the ACT Program and feel competent to begin teaching students from diverse urban backgrounds.

PROGRAM AND TEACHER RETENTION

During ACT's three years of implementation (98–01), 191 teacher candidates participated in the program, devoting a year to pre-service education. Of these candidates, 164 (86%) have received a credential, and 14 (7%) are in the process of completing a credential (see Table 3). It is anticipated that 178 of the teacher candidates initially enrolled in ACT will complete the program, a retention rate of 93%. Eleven students have withdrawn from the program, with the majority recruited for a teaching position and joining intern or traditional programs. Two students were exited from the program because of poor academic and/or classroom performance.

TABLE 3 Recruitment/Retention of ACT Candidates, 1998–2001					
Credential Area	Number Recruited	Number/% Receiving Credential	Number/% Continuing	Number/% Who Withdrew	Number Exited
Elementary	80	73 (91%)	5 (6%)	1 (1%)	1 (1%)
Secondary	59	51 (86%)	2 (3%)	6 (10%)	
Special Education	52	40 (77%)	7 (13%)	4 (8%)	1 (2%)
Total	191	164 (86%)	14 (7%)	11 (7%)	2 (1%)

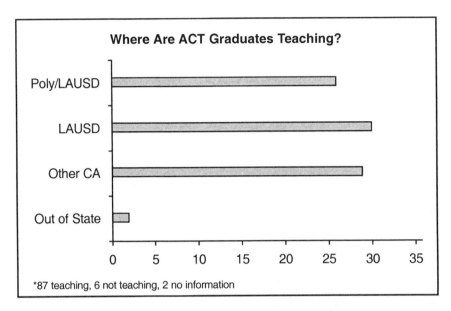

Figure 3. Placement of ACT Graduates

Ninety-two percent of ACT graduates who completed the program in 1999 and 2000 are teaching, with about one-third in the Poly Family in LAUSD, one-third in other schools in LAUSD, and one-third in other school districts in California (See Figure 3). Twelve of the fourteen Polytechnic Schools have hired at least one ACT graduate. Findings from these data suggest that teacher candidates who enter the ACT program are likely to complete the program, with the majority teaching in the Poly Family and other high-need areas of LAUSD. Thus, the ACT Program is directly contributing to the need for qualified teachers in urban Los Angeles and to other schools in California.

In the year 2000, the ACT program was recognized by two professional organizations as exemplifying a school/university partnership in the preparation of teachers:

- The *Urban Impact Award*, from the Council of Great City Colleges of Education
- The *Quality of Education Award for Distinguished Service to Children and Preparation of Teachers*, from the California Council on the Education of Teachers

Implications for Teacher Education Reform

Our experiences in creating the ACT program suggest that innovative models of teacher preparation can promote the recruitment, preparation, and retention of teachers for urban schools. However, we have learned that restructuring teacher education provides many challenges. As shown in Table 4, many of these challenges were addressed by restructuring the preparation program to provide school-university collaborative positions, support recruitment activities, promote collaborative planning and teaching, and incorporate evaluation as an integral program component that guides program decisions. Clearly, a quality program requires resources that support and promote school-university coordination and collaboration. Through the ACT Program, we have learned the following lessons that can help inform practices in teacher education.

RECRUITMENT AND SUPPORT

It is very challenging to recruit students into a one-year program, given the number of teaching positions available for individuals with emergency certification. We learned that recruitment must include a comprehensive system of strategies, advertising the unique features of the program and the advantages in preparation prior to teaching. Participants were also attracted to the program through financial support (stipends, fee waivers, loans, part-time work), individualized advisement, availability of courses, mentoring, and cohort participation.

SCHOOL-UNIVERSITY COLLABORATION

Schools and universities have their own unique cultures. To facilitate collaborative work and mutual trust, cross-institutional positions were established in which K–12 and university faculty coordinated the program, working with faculty to develop a common vision, program goals, and activities. These positions were essential in developing and sustaining school-university collaboration. The ACT Coordinators have become what Sandholtz and Finan (1998) call *border spanners,* crossing school and university cultures and becoming more knowledgeable and comfortable in either culture. With increasing time demands, Coordinators each took distinctive leadership roles in budget matters, as a liaison with the funding agency and institution, in curriculum coordination, and in communication with departments and schools. Significant resources, paid initially through grant funding and then

TABLE 4

ACT Program Major Challenges and Solutions

Challenges	Solutions
Develop a collaborative among school and university partners	Cross-institutional positions and school-university committees were established to govern and guide the collaborative.
Develop a program that provides best practices in teacher preparation for urban schools	Program Coordinators conducted a needs assessment with school, community, and university groups, and reviewed research on teacher preparation. Faculty, teachers, and administrators worked together and met frequently in cooperative teams to design the program.
Structure differentiated roles and responsibilities for participants with program decisions made collaboratively	Each University Coordinator served as a liaison in their respective departments; the PreK–12 Coordinator coordinated activities with the school family.
Facilitate program coordination through collaborative planning and teaching	Collaborative planning meetings were an integral part of the program and included weekly coordinator meetings, weekly core planning meetings, and a meeting in each module involving all ACT faculty.
Build collaborative time among university faculty and school personnel within the organized structure	The university provided collaborative time for core faculty, and grant funds were used to support coordinators.
Identify organizational structures needed to redesign the program and develop strategies	Program Coordinators implemented internal and external evaluation procedures and used student comments to guide program practice.
Generate administrative support at the university and district level	Program Coordinators and ACT faculty emphasized quality credentialing as a solution to the state and national teacher shortage and suggested an option to alternative programs.

supported in part by the university, fund these coordinator positions. Without such support for coordination and program management, it is unlikely that school-university partnerships can succeed (Burstein et al., 1999).

COLLABORATIVE PLANNING AND TEACHING

Faculty members typically work alone rather than together. Given little collaboration, there is often redundancy or gaps in coursework. In the ACT Program, faculty across departments and with K–12 teachers collaboratively plan and implement the program. This collaborative effort has resulted in faculty from different departments in the College of Education working closely together and with K–12 colleagues. Collaborative planning and teaching was supported financially, with units allocated to university faculty to support collaboration and stipends provided to K–12 personnel. This commitment of resources for collaboration was a critical component of restructuring, providing critical time for faculty to work with one another.

EMPHASIS ON DIVERSITY

Preparing teachers to meet the needs of students from low-income families, diverse in culture and language, requires ongoing program attention and emphasis. In the ACT Program, content focusing on diverse and urban learners was incorporated across the curriculum, continually revisited as new content and themes were introduced, and directly linked to teacher candidates' fieldwork in urban schools. Strategies in teaching the content were discussed among faculty throughout the program. Through this process, faculty shared their knowledge and learned from one another, developing expertise in teaching about diverse urban learners.

CLINICAL PREPARATION

Consistently, research indicates the importance of ongoing clinical preparation in learning to teach. In the ACT Program, fieldwork was designed to increase over time and transition teacher candidates from observing and participating to teaching. Clinical preparation was completed with exemplary teachers, trained as coaches, who also participated in coursework through lesson demonstration and team teaching. These experiences were highly valued by program participants, supporting the need for quality field-based experiences that are closely linked with coursework.

EVALUATION

A critical factor in the success of the ACT Program has been the incorporation of evaluation as an integral part of the collaborative effort to restructure teacher education. Ongoing program evaluation has informed program practices and assisted in revising curriculum and teaching strategies.

Summary

The ACT Program focuses on meeting the needs of diverse urban learners by providing qualified teachers for urban schools. The program is structured to facilitate school-university collaboration through cross-institutional coordinator positions, collaborative planning and teaching, field-based experiences with diverse urban learners, and ongoing evaluation that informs program practices. Offering a viable alternative to predominant teacher preparation models, ACT plays a vital role in the local community, contributing qualified teachers to schools who are most in need. The ACT program's model of collaboration and partnership serves as a bright, positive light in teacher education, both in California and the nation.

REFERENCES

Archer, J. (1999, March 17). New Teachers Abandon Field at High Rate. *Education Week, 18* (27), 1, 16, 21.

Artiles, A.J. & Trent, S.C. (1994). Over-Representation of Minority Students in Special Education: A Continuing Debate. *Journal of Special Education, 27*(4), 410–437.

Berry, B. (2000). Quality Alternatives in Teacher Preparation: Dodging the Silver Bullet and Doing What Is Right. *Welcome to the State Education Standards.* Paper prepared for the National Commission on Teaching and America's Future, Kutztown, PA.

Bullough, R.V., Hobbs, S.F., Kauchak, D.P., Crow, N.A., & Stokes, D. (1997). Long-Term PDS Development in Research Universities and the Clinicalization of Teacher Education. *Journal of Teacher Education, 48*(2), 85–95.

Burstein, N., Cabello, B., & Hamann, J. (1993). Teacher Preparation for Culturally Diverse Urban Students: Infusing Competencies Across the Curriculum. *Teacher Education and Special Education, 16*(1), 1–13.

Burstein, N., Kretschmer, D., Smith, C., & Gudoski, P. (1999). Redesigning Teacher Education as a Shared Responsibility of Schools and Universities. *Journal of Teacher Education, 50*(2), 106–118.

Carnegie Forum on Education and the Economy (1986). *A Nation Prepared: Teachers for the 21st Century.* New York: Author.

Center for the Future of Teaching and Learning. (1999). *Teaching and California's Future.* SRI International, Santa Cruz, CA: Author.

Chiang, S. (1998, August 9). CSUN offers Accelerated Course. *Daily News,* pp. A3, A6.

Darling-Hammond, L. (1996). What Matters Most: A Competent Teacher for Every Child. *Phi Delta Kappan, 76,* 193–200.

Darling-Hammond, L. (2000). How Teacher Education Matters. *Journal of Teacher Education, 51*(3), 166–173.

Darling-Hammond, L., & McLaughlin, M.W. (1995). Policies that Support Professional Development in an Era of Reform. *Phi Delta Kappan, 76,* 597–604.

Edwards, H. (2001, September 17). LAAMP Lights Students' Way. *Daily News,* p. A4.

Fullan, M. (1994). *Change Forces: Probing the Depths of Educational Reform.* New York: Falmer.

Genzuk, M., Lavadenz, M., & Krashen, S. Para-Educators: A Source for Remedying the Shortage of Teachers for Limited-English Proficient Students. *The Journal of Educational Issues of Language Minority Students, 14,* 211–222.

Grant, C.A. (1994). Best Practices in Teacher Preparation for Urban Schools: Lessons from the Multicultural Teacher Education Literature. *Action in Teacher Education, 14*(3), 1–18.

Hardman, M. (Ed.). (1997). *Building Partnerships: Preparing Special Education Teachers for the 21st Century.* Washington, DC: Joseph P. Kennedy Jr. Foundation in Collaboration with the Office of Special Education Programs, U.S. Department of Education.

Harry, B., Rueda, R., & Kalyanpur, M. (1999). Cultural Reciprocity in Sociocultural Perspective: Adapting the Normalization Principle for Family Collaboration. *Exceptional Children, 66,* 123–136.

Hart, G.K., & Burr, S.K. (1996). *The Teachers Who Teach Our Teachers: Teacher Preparation Programs at the California State University.* Sacramento, CA: The CSU Institute for Education Reform.

Hirsch, E. (2001). *The Impact of Teacher Quality.* Presentation to the California Commission on Teacher Credentialing, Title II Summer 2001 Workshop: Focus on SB2042.

Holmes Group. (1986). *Tomorrow's Schools: Principles for the Design of Professional Development Schools*. East Lansing, MI: Author.

Huling, L., Resta, V., & Rainwater, N. (2001). The Case for a Third Alternative: One University's Trip. *Journal of Teacher Education, 52*(4), 326–338.

Kagan, D.M. (1992). Professional Growth Among Pre-Service and Beginning Teachers. *Review of Educational Research, 62*(2), 129–169.

Kleinasser, A.M., & Paradis, E.E. (1997). Changing Teacher Education in the Context of a School-University Partnership: Disrupting Temporal Organizational Arrangement. *Teacher Education Quarterly, 24*(2), 63–73.

Kochan, F.K., & Kunkel, R.C. (1998). The Learning Coalition: Professional Development Schools in Partnership. *Journal of Teacher Education, 49*(5), 325–333.

Ladson-Billings, G. (1995). Multicultural teacher Education: Research, Practice, and Policy. In J.A. Banks & C.A. McGee Banks (Eds.), *Handbook of Research on Multicultural Education* (pp. 747–739). New York: MacMillan.

McAllister, G. & Irvine, J.J. (2000). Cross-Cultural Competency and Multicultural Teacher Education. *Review of Educational Research, 70*(1), 3–24.

Metcalf-Turner, P., & Fischetti, J. (1996). Professional Development Schools: Persisting Questions and Lessons Learned. *Journal of Teacher Education, 47*(2), 292–299.

Obiakor, F.E. & Schwenn, J.O. (1996). Assessment and Culturally Diverse Students with Behavior Disorders. In A.F. Rotatori, J.O. Schwenn, & S. Burkardt (Eds.), *Advances in Special education: Assessment and Psychopathology Issues in Special Education* (Vol. 10, pp 37–57). Greenwich, CT: JAI Press.

Obiakor, F.E. & Utley, C.A. (1997). Rethinking Pre-Service Preparation for Teachers in the Learning Disabilities Field: Workable Multicultural Strategies. *Learning Disabilities Research & Practice, 12*(2), 100–106.

Otis-Wilborn, A., & Winn, J. (2000). The Process and Impact of Standards-Based Teacher Education Reform. *Teacher Education and Special Education, 23*(2), 78–92.

Pleasants, A.M., Johnson, C.B., & Trent, S.C. (1998). Reflecting, Reconceptualizing, and Revising: The Evolution of a Portfolio Assignment in a Multicultural Teacher Education Course. *Remedial and Special Education, 19*, 46–58.

Rigden, D.W. (1996). What Teachers Have to Say about Teacher Education. *Perspective: Council for Basic Education, 8*(1), 18.

Sandholtz, J.H., & Finan, E.C. (1998). Blurring the Boundaries to Promote School-University Partnerships. *Journal of Teacher Education, 49*(1), 13–25.

Shanker, A. (1996). Quality Assurance: What Must Be Done to Strengthen the Teaching Profession. *Phi Delta Kappan, 78,* 220–224.

Soto, G., & Goetz, L. (1998). Self-Efficacy Beliefs and the Education of Students with Severe Disabilities. *Journal for the Association of Persons with Severe Handicaps, 23,* 134–143.

U.S. Department of Education (1998). *Promising Practices: New Ways to Improve Teacher Quality.* Washington, DC: Author.

Veal, M.L. & Rikard, L. (1998). Cooperating Teachers' Perspectives on the Student Teaching Triad. *Journal of Teacher Education,49*(2), 108–119.

Villegas, A.M., Clevell, B.C., Anderson, B.T., Goertz, M.D., Joy, M.F., Bruchi, B.A., & Irvine, J.J. (1995). *Teaching for Diversity: Models for Expanding the Supply of Minority Teachers.* Princeton, NJ: Educational Testing Service.

Voltz, D.L., Dooley, E. & Jeffries, P. (1999). Preparing Special Educators for Cultural Diversity: How Far Have We Come? *Teacher Education and Special Education, 22*(1), 66–77.

Wideen, M., Mayer-Smith, J., & Moon, B. (1998). A Critical Analysis of the Research on Learning to Teach: Making the Case for an Ecological Perspective on Inquiry. *Review of Educational Research, 68*(2), 130–178.

Winitzsky, N., Stoddard, T., & O'Keefe, P. (1992). Great Expectations: Emergent Professional Development Schools. *Journal of Teacher Education, 43*(2), 3–18.

Winzer, M.A. & Mazuerek, K. (1998). *Special Education in Muticultural Contexts.* Upper Saddle River, NJ: Prentice Hall.

Summary

Charles Watson and Emma M. Savage-Davis

T he two chapters in this section discuss issues surrounding the preparation of pre-service teachers for teaching in urban areas. In the first chapter, Alder provides an interesting and important literature-based framework that explores five primary areas of focus for educating pre-service teachers to teach in high poverty schools. The first focus area suggests using community service learning experiences as a means to explore and broaden pre-service teachers' awareness and understanding of school populations in impoverished areas. Furthermore, this focus area suggests community service learning as a primary vehicle to help pre-service teachers modify beliefs, values, attitudes, and overall perceptions and stereotypes of children and schools in impoverished areas. That is, the chapter implies that pre-service teachers often hold a "deficit" model of children and schools in urban areas, and these beliefs should be changed to reflect beliefs founded on equality and equity. A concentrated service learning experience can be critical to altering belief systems.

The second focus area builds on the community service learning concept by adding the valuable component of reflection. Through guided reflection, pre-service teachers can therefore extend the positions held in their own belief system, and base their commitment on an actual diverse experience, as well as accurately visualize their position within a particular diverse educational setting. As pre-service teachers contemplate their own life and experiences in the contexts of educational and social philosophies and the purpose of schooling in a democratic society, they can formulate and develop greater sensitivity for populations and cultures different from their own and therefore become much more aware of how they will fit within those environments. Reflection is known to bring more wealth and understanding to newly found knowledge of any experience for pre-service teachers.

The third focus area further expands the need for teachers' awareness of historical, socioeconomic, cultural and political factors that influence poverty. The author suggests that inequality of educational opportunity reaches deeper than simple curricular issues, and that the problem stems from the historical and political impact of minority communities and how that affects the funding mechanism of schools and therefore quality. As populations shift and become more diverse, businesses flee to the suburbs, and the tax base and financial support for education are quickly reduced. Furthermore, the changes in the populations occurred as a result of attempts to desegregate the school systems in urban areas. The chapter discusses the correlation among these changes in the population, the reductions of available funds and the historical impact on tracking students in urban areas, including the overrepresentation of minority students in lower, special education, and vocational tracks.

The fourth focus area of the Alder chapter is directed toward preparing teachers to be active and thoughtful in praxis, practice and responsiveness, enabling them to make positive changes in high poverty schools. Teachers must understand how to help bring about empowerment, both for themselves and for their students if they are to effectively participate in a democracy and take responsibility for their own learning, including learning personal and academic skills. Teachers must also make learning relevant to the students' lives in order to enhance students' knowledge potential both within the context of schooling and in students' non-school lives. Furthermore, curriculum and other educational materials should be reflective of the student population and teaching methods should support multiple learning styles. That is, the learning environments must be enriched, culturally supportive, and filled with expert teaching practices.

The fifth and final focus area is improving the awareness of models of comprehensive educational change, reform, and restructuring models that are prevalent in high poverty schools. These models are wide-ranging and can vary from action research and needs assessment to reading improvement or classroom management improvement, but most all have the common goal of providing support for students who are academically behind. In addition, these models are not generally found as aspects of traditional (or alternative) licensure and teacher preparation programs. Instead, most programs focus on discrete skill sets and content knowledge. Because these comprehensive school reform models are so predominant in urban schools, any teacher education program directed toward improving educational opportunities and achievement in urban schools would be remiss if some degree of study about these models was not present in urban teachers' preparation. The Alder chapter suggests that within the context of any of these models, the notion of developing school learning communities is crucial to any reform effort, and thus preparation for teaching in urban settings should help new teachers not only become a part of learning communities, but help them develop such communities; learning communities offer deeply woven relationships that lend themselves to improved educational learning environments.

In the second chapter, Lombardi, Smith, Burstein and Cunningham describe an alternative preparation program in California that focuses on recruitment and retention of teachers for teaching in diverse schools. The chapter describes the Accelerated Collaborative Teacher (ACT) program, begun in1995 in a diverse, urban school district of the San Fernando Valley of California.

The program focuses on three primary and unambiguous objectives: recruitment, preparation, and retention of teachers in and for an urban diverse setting. The program seeks to restructure teacher education and prepare teachers for teaching in diverse settings through a standards-based curriculum and field-based teacher preparation program. In an effort to provide help for new teachers in what was earlier described as daunting, the program provides content and experiences related to special needs learners, multicultural education, bilingual education, instructional technology, educational psychology, and educational leadership. The program was established by a collaborative relationship between four PreK–12 schools and a state university in California, with professional development centers established at each school; in most cases, these schools were experiencing low test scores and higher than normal level of emergency credentialed teachers. As noted in the previous sections, emergency credentialed teachers often leave the profession at higher rates and earlier than traditionally prepared teachers, and are often ill-prepared to meet the challenges of teaching in urban or high poverty schools. In one school, the effects of this resulted in 80% of high school graduates unprepared for college-level courses.

The chapter also suggests there is often a disconnection between universities and K–12 school districts in many respects, including poor quality of student teaching experiences, weak links between schools of education and liberal studies, limited early clinical experiences, and lack of shared responsibility for student achievement.

The ACT program seeks to address those problems and to provide experiences and coursework and makes powerful links between theory and practice. Program university faculty and classroom teachers were trained as teachers/coaches for the program to share their knowledge and bridge theory and practice in courses that are team-taught. This collaborative teaching approach spanned elementary, secondary and special education levels and allowed program faculty to build excellent, content-rich courses and experiences for candidates. The ACT program consists of thirty-six credit hours in a core curriculum, specialized courses for elementary, secondary, and special education curriculum, and field experiences aligned to both the core and specialized courses, as well as other state and university requirements. Throughout the program teacher candidates develop a portfolio of lesson plans, student samples, and other artifacts from the experiences to document competency of the California Standards for the Teaching Profession. In addition, the program accelerates the process of licensure, making it a worthwhile substitute for emergency credentialing.

Collaboration and shared commitment from both university and school district administrations were crucial. Periodically leaders from both university (ACT Coordinators) and K–12 schools (Practitioner Team Leaders) meet to plan and make decisions regarding the various aspects of the program. Early results appear very promising. In the first three years of implementation, 86% of the 191 teacher candidates completed the program and received credentials, 7% were in the process of completing their credentials. Eleven percent withdrew from the program, with the majority being recruited for teaching positions or other programs, and only two students exited from the program because of academic and/or classroom performance.

As a result of these assessments, the ACT program, originally implemented on an experimental basis, has now been approved for permanent status and has been recognized as exemplary by two professional organizations for its school/university partnership in teacher preparation.

This chapter highlights one successful program for preparing teachers that is competitive with other alternative methods of certification but maintains the quality and dignity of teacher preparation. This successful program could possibly be seen as a framework for other teacher preparation programs in this time of alternative routes to certification, and the recent federal legislation calling for all teachers to be "highly qualified."

Both chapters address a central theme: preparing teachers for teaching in impoverished, diverse, and urban areas. The problems associated with urban and high poverty schools are vast and enormously complex; however, they are not isolated or relegated to schools, school buildings, and school districts. Indeed, the problems extend deeply into urban as well as some rural cultures, and are interrelated with the nation's historic, political, and economic past, present, and future, as ably noted in the first chapter, and described widely in educational literature. The chapters are descriptive because they provide a beginning basis for comprehensive approaches and an excellent example of a method that is having admirable results.

Division

3

Educators Working in Culturally Diverse Schools

Educators Working in Culturally Diverse Schools
Linking Colleges of Education and Partnership Schools

6.

Edwina Battle Vold and Jyotsna Pattnaik

Edwina Battle Void is Professor Emerita at Indiana University of Pennsylvania. Her research and publications focus on education that is multicultural and early childhood education.

Jyotsna Pattnaik is Associate Professor at the University of California, Long Beach. Her research interests are in early childhood education, multicultural education and global child advocacy.

ABSTRACT

The framework for the research studies in this section of the yearbook, including the introduction, embrace the work of varied theorists and researchers (Ahlquist, 1991; Banks, 1989; Pattnaik and Vold, 1994, 1998, 1999; Sleeter and Grant, 1988). The research addresses issues of preparing teachers for diverse schools but also factors that promote greater communication between teacher education institutions and public schools as they endeavor to embrace differences and promote equity. Throughout our nation's history, there have been some schools, including some high-poverty schools in our urban and rural communities, that have responded to issues of diversity, social change, social welfare and reform in addition to being the purveyor of knowledge, skills and behaviors necessary for an informed citizenry. The research studies in this section offer us a glimpse of some of those schools, teachers and programs.

Introduction and Framework

Colleges and universities engaged in the preparation of teachers have a central role in the positive development of our culturally pluralistic society. If cultural pluralism is to become an integral part of the education process, teachers (for culturally diverse schools) must be prepared in an environment where the commitment to multicultural education is evident. . . . Multicultural education programs for teachers are more than special courses or special learning experiences grafted onto the standard program. The commitment to cultural pluralism must permeate all areas of the educational experience provided for prospective teachers (AACTE, 1970, p. 264).

AACTE's statement, No One Model American, states the need for teacher education institutions to actively initiate programs for preparing teachers to teach in culturally diverse schools. It calls for a commitment on the part of all constituents including public school personnel who do not often see themselves as teacher educators. It calls for a holistic rather than fragmented approach to the knowledge-base and structured field experiences in settings that are culturally different from that of the pre-service teacher. That is why we have chosen to use a condensed version of our study on 'Perceptions and Practices of Pre-service and In-service Teachers Working in Culturally Diverse Schools' as an introduction to this section on Educators Working in Culturally Diverse Schools.

The research study on perceptions and practices of pre-service and in-service teachers, is part of a series of research studies in the genre of education that is multicultural. The study, as does the three research studies in this section, reflects our moral and ethical responsibility to prepare teachers who are able to respond to all kinds of diversity and especially to the dynamics of power and privilege that nurture, sustain and legitimate inequities (Weis & Fine, 1993).

The study occurred as the College of Education was responding to issues of diversity in structure and policy. In the Department of Professional Studies in Education, we were engaged in reform efforts to more effectively infuse multicultural concepts into the undergraduate curriculum and to expand the field experiences to include inner city/urban schools as partners. It was believed that the expanded field experiences would have an impact on the 'cultural baggage' that many of our pre-service teachers bring with them to the teacher preparation program (Mills & Buckley, 1992).

The multicultural competencies collaboratively developed by the faculty included knowledge, skills and attitudes and were systematically included into specific required courses for the pre-service teachers. The faculty also developed and approved a Multicultural Ethnic Studies Policy Statement that served as a catalyst for dialogue and conversation on the processes and the products and our beliefs about multicultural education theories and practices. There were some notable clefts in the reform efforts. There was no conversation with faculty in the liberal arts who deliver more that two-thirds of coursework or with faculty in our partnership schools who have the major responsibility of evaluating the practices that are reflective of the theories taught. Without these colleagues involved in the reform process, the possibility of disconnect and fragmentation loomed large.

The reformed program embodied a number of ideas pertinent to teaching including ideas about *equity in education* and *reflectivity in teaching*. They were intersecting factors that were fundamental to our understanding of the quantity and quality of education practices that support multicultural education, especially in our partnership schools.

With regard to *equity in education*, the department stated that its teachers in preparation and those with whom we partner in public schools must be committed to ensuring equitable access to and participation in the best possible education for all children. This includes advocating for children of varying abilities, varying socio-economic needs, and cultural and linguistic backgrounds (Goodlad, 1991). With regard to *reflectivity* in teaching the department stated that its teachers in preparation must reflect on teaching individually and in collaboration with colleagues. They need time to reflect on classroom experiences; using information to make informed judgements, and to modify strategies accordingly (Eby, 1992).

The partnership schools were selected based on 'history' but also because we found a need to diversify the field experiences providing our pre-service teachers with the opportunities to be immersed in schools and communities with which they were not always familiar with or comfortable in. In all of the partnership schools, faculty and cooperating teachers had joint responsibility for providing a comprehensive educational experience to improve the curriculum, instruction, and evaluation for all children. The partnership schools, especially the inner-city/urban school where courses were taught 'on-site, provided the department with additional expertise. These cooperating teachers were as experts in pedagogy and management reflective of the realistic practices that often did not mirror the theories conveyed in on-campus coursework.

As stated by McIntyre (1979), the use of partnership schools for field experiences helps to facilitate the integration of theory and practice. In fact, the underlying construct within the partnership school/university relationship, is that the theories and practices of the department and those of the school would be similar with regard to what is to be taught, to whom and that both constituents would be committed to strategies that were appropriate for all children.

It was because of this underlying construct and our belief in the partner school concept that the researchers posed the following questions with regard to equity and congruence and used them to remain focused throughout the semester long study.

- Do the experiences in the departmental program correspond to the multicultural education goals as specified in the self-study and other documents for external review?
- Will there be differences in the beliefs about diversity and the multicultural practices of pre-service and in-service teachers in rural, urban and suburban partnership schools?
- Is there congruence between the on-campus experiences and the expected competencies in field experiences in the partnership schools?

Purposes of the Study

The purposes of the research study were to determine:

1. what occurs in student teachers' classrooms with cooperating teachers with regard to instruction that is appropriate for children of various cultures, various abilities, various socio-economic levels and gender;
2. the types of activities that student teachers create within their lesson plans that support the theories and content of multicultural education;
3. if pre-service teachers and their in-service cooperating teachers, through reflection, are able to determine the consistencies and inconsistencies that exists between their beliefs and practices; and
4. if in-service teachers in the partnerships schools and the departmental faculty believe in education that is multicultural and advocate for the pre-service teachers by supporting their use of multicultural instructional materials and strategies.

The population for the research study included student teachers from the department, cooperating teachers and faculty supervisors from three selected partnership schools in rural, suburban and urban communities. Fourteen student teachers and fourteen cooperating teachers volunteered and took part in the initial assessment. Two of the fourteen teachers were dropped from the study because of assignments outside of the classroom and thus their student teachers were also dropped from the study. The final sample population consisted of 5 student teachers and cooperating teachers in the urban school, three student teachers and cooperating teachers in the rural school, and four student teachers and cooperating teachers in the suburban school. The student teachers were Caucasian and female. Of the twelve cooperating teachers, one was male and one was African American.

Methodology

Ethnography, as a research tool, was used to collect data. It allowed the researcher and assistants to describe the complex behaviors and practices of multiple constituents. There was no attempt to compare or contrast behaviors or practices—only to describe what we observed systematically. Thus, we were able to learn from the student teachers and the cooperating teachers as they shared what they knew and what they believed they were doing. An opinionnaire designed for a Multicultural Teacher as Education Project at a historically Black University, and the modified checklists that had been used in an earlier pilot study were the major instruments. The questions for the post-interview used with pre-service and in-service teachers were modified from previous studies by Pattnaik (1994). The researchers visited each pre-service and in-service teacher together to ensure inter-rater reliability in the techniques, practices observed and the reflections shared.

Analysis of Data Summary

With regard to the questions asked:

1. the opinions, perceptions and practices garnered from instruments, and observations do not reflect the perceived experiences and stated mission of the department with regard to education that is multicultural;
2. the pre-service and in-service teachers in the partnership schools did differ from student teachers in suburban and rural schools with regard to multicultural practices although a majority of the content centered around African-American and other white ethnic groups;
3. the practices observed tended to adhere more to the contributions and additive approaches without any commitment to education that is multicultural or instructional strategies that were systematically infused into the curriculum; and
4. the student teachers from the urban school were more effective in recognizing consistencies and inconsistencies in their beliefs and practices. This may have occurred more frequently because the reflective thinking

practices were not a novel process since they engaged in reflection weekly with the university supervisor assigned to that school.

Conclusion

Student teaching experiences have great meaning for most pre-service teachers beyond the structure and skills learned. It is a phase of their professional development that allows them to formulate a raison d'etre and to become oriented to the reality of molding the lives of children from diverse student populations. The findings in this study and those studies that follow raise questions about the development of effective strategies for multicultural teacher education. These questions center around three of the themes in the following chapters: diversity, collaboration, and systemic reform. For many in-service teachers, responding to educational policies that require the inclusion of content on diversity involves learning new practices. This requires in-service teachers and many pre-service teachers to incorporate teaching practices reflective of diversity into their instructional repertoire and adapting these practices into existing pedagogical understandings (Montecinos & Tidwell, 1996). What is recommended is the promotion of systemic approaches to matters of content and to pedagogy in interactive, supportive environments in which philosophic objectives and difficulties can be worked out collaboratively.

Ziechner (1983) has suggested that during the student teaching experience, pre-service and in-service teachers alike must examine the consequences of their actions within the settings in which they work. With the changing demographics of the present and future populations, Ziechner's suggestions are more than ever a necessary skill for all prospective teachers and more of an impetus to systematically design teacher education programs that are theoretically sound and grounded in practices that support the realities that individuals experience in culturally diverse and complex encounters.

REFERENCES

Ahlquist, R. (1991). Position and Imposition: Power Relations in a Multicultural Foundations Class. *Journal of Negro Education, 60*(2), 158–169.

American Association of Colleges for Teacher Education (1970). No One Model America: A Statement on Multicultural Education. *Journal of Teacher Education, 24*, 264.

Banks, J. A. (1989). Integrating the Curriculum with Ethnic Content: Approaches and Guidelines. In J. A. Banks & Banks, C. M. (Eds.), *Multicultural Education: Issues and Perspectives* (pp. 189–207). Boston: Allyn & Bacon.

Eby, J. W. (1992). *Reflective Planning, Teaching, and Evaluation for the Elementary School.* New York: Macmillan.

Goodlad, J. I. (1991). *Teachers for Our Nation's Schools.* San Francisco: Jossey-Bass.

McIntyre, D. J. (1979). Integrating Theory and Practice Via Teaching Center. *Contemporary Education, 50*(3), 146–149.

Mills, J. R. & Buckley, C. W. (1992). Accommodating the Minority Teacher Candidate: Non-Black Students in Predominantly Black Colleges. In M. E. Dilworth (Ed.), *Diversity in Teacher Education* (pp. 134–159). San Francisco, CA: Jossey-Bass.

Montecinos, C. & Tidwell, D. L. (1996). Teachers' Choices for Infusing Multicultural Content: Assimilating Multicultural Practices into Schemata for Instruction in the Content Area. In F. A. Rios (Ed.), *Teacher Thinking in Cultural Contexts* (pp. 230–245). Albany, NY: State University of New York Press.

Pattnaik, J. & Vold, E. B. (1994, February). *A Study of Student Teachers' Perceptions and Practices of Multicultural Education in School/University Partnerships.* Paper presented at Association of Teacher Educators National Conference, Atlanta, GA.

Pattnaik, J. & Vold, E. B. (1998). Pre-Service Teachers' Multicultural Literacy: Are We Missing the Forest for the Trees? *Equity and Excellence in Education, 31*(3), 73–84.

Pattnaik, J. & Vold, E. B. (1999). Expected Multicultural Education Outcomes in Teacher Education and the NCATE Factor. In E. B. Vold (Ed.), *Preparing Teachers for Diverse Student Populations and for Equity* (pp. 97–110). Dubuque, Iowa: Kendall/Hunt.

Vold, E. B. (1998). *Preparing Teachers for Diverse Student Populations and Equity.* Dubuque, Iowa: Kendall/Hunt.

Weis, L. & Fine, M. (1993). *Beyond Silenced Voices: Class, Race and Gender in United States Schools.* Albany, New York: State University of New York Press.

Zeichner, K. M. (1983). Alternative Paradigms of Teacher Education. *Journal of Teacher Education, 34*(3), 3–9.

Cooperating Teachers

7.

The Challenges of Teaching and Mentoring in Meeting the Needs of English Language Learners

Patricia Tate, Kris Anstrom, and Patricio Sanchez

Dr. Patricia Tate is Assistant Professor of Elementary Education in the Department of Teacher Preparation and Special Education and Director of the Office of Laboratory Experiences in the Graduate School of Education and Human Development at The George Washington University. Her research interests include technology in teacher education, teacher development, learning to teach, and clinical supervision.

Kristina Anstrom is the Project Director for Preparing All Administrators, Counselors and Teachers to Work with Linguistically and Culturally Diverse Students at the Institute for Education Policy Studies in the Graduate School of Education and Human Development at The George Washington University. Her research interests include ESL and bilingual education and mainstream instruction of English language learning students.

Patricio Sanchez is a Research Associate for Preparing All Administrators, Counselors and Teachers to Work with Linguistically and Culturally Diverse Students at the Institute for Education Policy Studies in the Graduate School of Education and Human Development at The George Washington University. His research interests include minority and diversity issues in higher education.

ABSTRACT

This study focuses on the needs of mainstream teachers who work with English language learning (ELL) students and their roles in mentoring interns to facilitate the learning of ELL students. The data informing this study were collected as part of an initiative to develop web-based support for cooperating teachers that addresses their teaching and mentoring with regard to working with ELL students. Participants were cooperating teachers from professional development and partnership schools of a private metropolitan university. Focus group sessions captured viewpoints and expressed needs. Data from these sessions were analyzed qualitatively. Data indicated that the major challenges of working with ELL students were: developing relationships with ELL students' families, instructing and assessing ELL students, and assisting in their transition to the mainstream. Researchers drew overarching themes related to challenges and successes in teaching ELL students and to mentoring teacher interns.

Objectives

This study focused on the needs of mainstream teachers who work with English language learning (ELL) students and their roles in mentoring interns to facilitate the learning of ELL students. Focus group sessions captured viewpoints and expressed needs of cooperating teachers who function in these roles. Participants were representatives from professional development schools and partner schools of a Graduate School of Education at a private metropolitan university. Data from these sessions were analyzed qualitatively and used in designing a web-based support system for cooperating teachers to access resources, information, and professional development experiences to support their teaching and mentoring with regard to ELL students.

The essential questions that framed this study were:

- What are the challenges and successes in working with ELL students in mainstream classrooms?
- What are the challenges and successes in mentoring interns to work with mainstreamed ELL students?

PROFESSIONAL DEVELOPMENT FOR MAINSTREAM TEACHERS OF ELL STUDENTS

The practice of "mainstreaming" ELL students before they develop the language proficiency necessary for all-English classroom work has been prevalent in our schools for some time. In fact, the majority of ELL students spend most of their school day with mainstream teachers (Ruiz-de-Velasco & Fix, 2000). Despite this phenomenon, scant research exists on mainstream teachers' needs relevant to the ELL student population. A research perspective that acknowledges mainstream teachers' classroom practices and knowledge relevant to ELL students provides an important context for initiating effective professional development programs.

Preparing teachers to educate ELL students in mainstream classrooms confirms what we know about teachers' professional development. It is most effective when it offers teachers opportunities to learn from peers and when it involves them in practice-based situations where they make decisions and take responsibility for their actions (Adger & Clair, 1999; Peredo, 1999). Professional development programs that increase ELL student learning focus on English instruction within key content areas, participant-centered activities, and the needs of first-year teachers (Adger & Clair, 1999; Peredo, 1999).

The small amount of literature aimed at mainstream teachers' work with ELL students indicates that professional development should support these teachers in becoming:

- mediators and facilitators of content learning (i.e., planning instruction that meets the academic and linguistic needs of ELL students),
- facilitators of English language acquisition (i.e., matching a particular teaching strategy with students' language skills, cognitive abilities, and content knowledge),
- models of proficient English language use (i.e., giving appropriate linguistic feedback),
- representatives of the mainstream culture (i.e., bridging the home and school's cultures), and
- advocates for ELL students (i.e., collaborating with other teachers and administrators on ELL students' education) (Carrasquillo & Rodriguez, 1996; Hamayan, 1990).

PREPARING PRE-SERVICE MAINSTREAM TEACHERS TO WORK WITH ELL STUDENTS

Teacher educators must support future teachers in developing the prerequisite competencies and dispositions necessary for working with ELL students. They include: understanding their own and others' sociocultural identities; validating differences in race, ethnicity and language; advocating for equitable schooling opportunities; viewing learning as a constructivist process; knowing their students well; and using instructional practices that bridge their knowledge of students with knowledge of teaching and learning (Villegas & Lucas, 2002).

An integral piece of the pre-service curriculum is the field-based experience. Of particular concern are the intern's classroom experiences with ELL students. The National Council for the Accreditation of Teacher Education (NCATE) devotes its fourth standard to the importance of teacher education programs providing "extensive and substantive" field experiences that "help candidates confront issues of diversity that affect teaching and student learning . . ." (NCATE, 2001, p. 31). NCATE's emphasis on the field experience is supported by studies showing that the internship and the cooperating teacher have the greatest impact on interns' development (Knowles & Cole, 1996; Glickman & Bey, 1990; Guyton & McIntyre, 1990). Efforts that assist interns in learning to work effectively with ELL students will help create a cadre of teachers supportive of ELL students' needs.

Methods

We used a qualitative approach to explore, capture, and analyze cooperating teachers' viewpoints and needs on their work with ELL students and on mentoring interns to work more effectively with ELL students.

SAMPLE AND PARTICIPANT SELECTION

Data were gathered from three focus group sessions with different participants during spring 2001. Participants were males and females with three to twenty-eight years of experience teaching in elementary, secondary, and special education settings. All sixteen participants came from university partner and professional development schools in a large metropolitan area. School principals assisted in identifying potential participants. Qualifications for participants included being (a) a university cooperating teacher with at least three years of mentoring experience, (b) a mainstream educator experienced in working with ELL students, and (c) willing to use technology.

DATA SOURCE

Researchers used focus groups to generate the data. The work of Flores and Alonso (1995) supported the use of focus groups to collect data when very little is known about a problem. As stated previously, scant research exists on mainstream teachers' needs relevant to the ELL student population.

A common protocol was used to collect written and oral data across the focus groups. Questions concerned the challenges of mentoring/supervision roles and how technology could address those challenges; the challenges of working with ELL students in mainstream classrooms; support structures that could address the identified challenges; technologies that could assist with mentoring interns; and mentoring mainstream teacher interns to work effectively with ELL students.

Focus groups were audio and video taped, then transcribed. Flip charts were used to document participants' major dialog sequences. The data set consisted of written reflections, flip chart data, and transcripts from all three focus groups.

As participants in two grant initiatives, researchers were facilitators and participant observers during the data collection process. The principal investigator was a university faculty member and Director of the Office of Laboratory Experiences, which places and monitors the supervision of interns. The second and third authors were a grant project director and research associate who were doctoral students at the university sponsoring the research.

DATA ANALYSIS

Data analysis involved "collaborative coding" (Glaser & Strauss, 1967) defined as a process of open dialogue and examination of the researchers' perspectives in interpreting rich data. Coding was holistic for "dialogue sequences", defined as one individual's response. A dialogue sequence could be coded for more than one category.

Researchers met weekly to share emerging themes and to develop the coding schema for the data. Dialogue examples representing these themes were recorded and assembled under dominant categories for each focus group. As patterns of dominant categories emerged across the three groups the researchers came to agreement about deleting, collapsing, and redefining categories. Category testing continued until consistency and alignment of categories were achieved. A coding guideline book was developed with specific examples from the data.

Researchers independently coded all data using coding guidelines. A tally process for each coding category was used to determine the most predominant themes across all data types. The themes became analytical constructs (Erikson, 1986) for summarizing results and interpreting the overarching ideas.

Results

The constructs that emerged from this study related to the research questions regarding challenges and successes experienced by participants. These constructs are described with examples from the data followed by researchers' interpretations of what was learned.

CHALLENGES IN WORKING WITH ENGLISH LANGUAGE LEARNING STUDENTS

The dominant themes that emerged from the data pertaining to the challenges of working with the ELL student were: developing relationships with ELL pupils' families, instructing ELL students and facilitating their content knowledge development, assessment, and transitioning to the mainstream.

Developing Relationships with ELL Students' Families

Participants realized that good communication with families is an integral part of student learning; they also acknowledged the challenge of communicating with parents from different language backgrounds. One participant spoke of the difficulty in having only a Spanish-speaking liaison person in the school when he worked with students and families from many language backgrounds.

Another challenge was understanding cultural factors that influenced the family-school relationship. When some of the participants criticized parents' lack of involvement in their children's education, one participant responded that involvement in schooling was culturally defined. In some cultures it was more appropriate not to get involved. Equally challenging was working with parents who disciplined their children in ways unacceptable in this country. Participants agreed that maltreatment, whether culturally-based or not, was unacceptable, but were unsure about how to broach the issue with parents from cultures that condoned such practices.

Instructing ELL Students and Facilitating Content Instruction

Teachers expressed frustration with the "trial and error" process of determining "what to teach first." They realized the diversity of ELL students' educational needs and noted the difficulty of teaching reading, oral language, and vocabulary to students whose English language proficiency levels and educational backgrounds varied greatly. The participants also expressed frustration with their attempts to teach abstract concepts through a second language.

The results indicated that the focus group teachers understood the challenges of educating ELL students but lacked the resources to work with these students in mainstream classrooms. This resource deficit was most keenly felt at the secondary level where the demands of teaching a set curriculum to as many as 150 students a day conflicted with ELL students' needs for individualized attention and a curriculum tailored to their language proficiency levels and previous experiences with the content.

Assessing ELL Students

Challenges related to assessment of ELL students concerned grading fairly under pressures from administrators to cover the curriculum. Additional concerns emerged about parental pressure regarding grading and placement of their child in English-as-a-second-language (ESL) classes.

Participants also felt it was difficult to assess true potential because of language issues. One participant commented: [The challenge is] "delivering the school required curriculum to the class and having ESL students succeed with the curriculum. In a grade-competitive classroom, non-ESL students challenge grading standards which are different for ESL students."

Participants also noted challenges in assessing ELL students who come to their classroom equipped with "survival English" but underdeveloped reading and writing skills. Participants expressed concern that the pressure of covering material for test preparation was leaving many ELL students behind.

Transitioning to the Mainstream Classroom

Two sub themes emerged within this category. The first concerned the lack of a "safety net" for mainstreamed ELL students. Some teachers believed that the change from ESL environments where class size is small to mainstream environments with large classes is difficult. Students used to receiving individualized attention from their ESL teachers struggled to learn with very little individualized attention and at more rapid paces. One teacher suggested a transition program. "They need to be able to come to class in the morning or afternoon, and then go back to another classroom where they get some more reinforcement and more practice."

The second sub theme within the transitioning category concerned ELL students and parents' perceptions of mainstream classroom learning as compared to ESL classroom learning. This theme can be summarized in the words of one participant: "If ESL kids get the idea that they're not getting the same stuff as the other kids are getting, they really resent it." Participants had also experienced parents refusing ESL services for their children and insisting that they be placed entirely in mainstream class-rooms.

Challenges in Mentoring Interns to Work with ELL Students

Challenges in facilitating interns' abilities to work effectively with ELL students were embedded within conversations about mentoring and supervision. Concerns related to this construct were assisting the intern in: building relationships with ELL students, assessing ELL students, and understanding the realities of classrooms with ELL students. The challenge identified for assisting the intern with building relationships involved how to encourage interns to be open with pupils and to trust that pupils will accept the intern as another learner.

Participants discussed their concerns about the importance of interns' understanding "there are no recipes in teaching." The basis of decisions about what to teach must begin with the assessed needs of the pupils. Our cooperating teachers felt strongly that interns must understand everything that makes up the assessment process not just data from paper-pencil tests, but also from daily observations. A comment captured this concern:

> The whole idea of flexibility [of the intern], that moment-to-moment we make a hundred little decisions that inform our teaching, I mean our observations, assessment. I have somebody [intern] now who's really looking at assessment. I think she means on paper, but I'm going to have to really explain that from the moment I meet a student I'm assessing all the time because that informs my teaching.

Participants focused on interns' lack of awareness of the "big picture" of the school in terms of student demographics and its influence on how curriculum is adapted. Concerns included interns' lack of awareness about their essential roles—to be committed to teaching the curriculum and adapting it to the needs of pupils as opposed to applying scripted lessons and strategies.

Cooperating teachers wanted university assistance in helping interns shift focus from scripted strategies and lesson plans to first understanding the students, then using that understanding to develop or select appropriate strategies: "With a new teacher, they're so intent on these lesson plans, because that's what they're being evaluated on, that we forget how many choices we provide our students. . . ." This comment underscores how the university's system of evaluating interns based on "performances" encourages them to display the strategies they know how to use rather than demonstrate their understanding of diverse learners' needs.

SUCCESSES IN TEACHING ENGLISH LANGUAGE LEARNING STUDENTS

A significant amount of dialogue captured successes related to teaching and assessing the ELL student in the mainstream classroom and to working and communicating with families. Successes were categorized as classroom level strategies that worked for all pupils or instructional adaptations useful for ELL students.

Successes at the classroom level included the use of cooperative groups in which ELL students could practice their oral skills and receive support from native English speakers, peer mentoring, and other structures that integrated different types of learners. The participants also discussed enhancing content delivery with visuals, "giving students the big picture" in ways that all students could understand, breaking instruction down into smaller chunks, and teaching study strategies. Learning centers that provided hands-on experiences in listening, speaking, reading, and writing were also recommended at the elementary level along with provision for a range of reading materials from "picture books to Harry Potter". Teachers emphasized the importance of using specific support services such as homework clubs.

In the category, "instructional adaptations," teachers discussed successes in pairing ELL students with a buddy who speaks the same language. They also discussed assigning ELL students to multilevel groups where those at higher levels mentor them. There were many examples of assisting the ELL students in organizing and completing their assignments by providing concrete structures such as color-coded folders and rubrics that represent the essential ideas and skills they must learn. They discussed teaching language by highlighting word origins, word relationships, and word use across many languages. With regard to assessment, participants discussed how they provided alternative ways for ELL students to demonstrate their learning through technology (i.e. web pages, overheads, audiotapes).

Participants stressed their work in involving parents in activities of interest to them through school and community centers. They mentioned the importance of native language speaking liaisons who established and maintained relations between the school and the home. Also important were native language materials for parents and ways of encouraging parents to share their language and culture.

OVERARCHING THEMES

Overarching themes were interpreted from the data that identified success-ful practices for working with ELL students and for mentoring interns to work with ELL students. These overarching themes were: learning about learners, providing appropriate instructional practices, and taking leader-ship as change agents and advocates.

Learning about Learners

The first overarching theme derived from the analytical constructs was the importance of mentoring interns to "learn about learners". Participants emphasized the importance of building bridges between the knowledge and experiences students bring from their families and cultures and the concepts and skills they must learn in school. The literature on working with diverse students confirmed that teachers who draw from the "funds of knowledge" students possess were better able to support their in-school learning experi-ences (Moll & Gonzalez, 1997).

Building relationships with ELL students and with their families in order to draw on students' "funds of knowledge" was important not only to their own teaching but also to their role as mentors of future teachers of ELL stu-dents. The first step in mentoring interns in this process was to encourage interns to develop relationships with individual students. One teacher remarked that the first thing she asked her intern to do was to spend time with individual students.

The teachers contrasted what they felt was important for interns to do to become "culturally responsive" (Villegas & Lucas, 2002) teachers of ELL students with what many interns thought they should be doing. Interns brought strategies and lesson plans from their university-based education courses that they wanted to try out in the classroom. The cooperating teach-ers were concerned about this disconnect between what the university had prepared them to do and what the realities of teaching ELL learners demanded.

Additionally, the participants viewed establishing relationships with lin-guistically and culturally diverse families as both a challenge and a neces-sity. They discussed the importance of understanding cultural factors that could influence the family-school relationship. Mentoring interns to develop the dispositions critical to establishing relationships with families and seek-ing knowledge of cultural factors involved modeling inquiry skills and seek-ing information through school, district and community resources. In the words of one participant, "I think a student intern needs to know why the family is not addressing the kids' needs." These examples demonstrated how participants communicated and modeled their role in using ELL students' knowledge and experiences to create a more meaningful learning environment for them.

Appropriate Instructional Practices

Participants attributed great importance to building classroom climate and establishing trust, honesty, and openness. Cooperating teachers discussed practices they modeled for an intern including: orienting their intern to the class and assisting in building rapport and positive relationships, starting curriculum planning and lesson design after assessment of pupils' needs and the content to be taught, and facilitating how pupils processed information and exhibited their learning.

Practices discussed for productive beginnings with pupils and interns encompassed employing a thoughtful approach to intern-pupil orientation and using this orientation as an opportunity to model establishing classroom community. One participant shared this practice:

> You know we have a big chat when the student intern comes, we sit down, everybody introduces himself or herself around the carpet, including the student intern, and I'll say—'In order for her to do the best teaching, what sort of cooperation does she need from you?' . . . I spend a lot of time the first few weeks building my classroom community.

Facilitating interns' understanding of how to adapt curriculum to meet the needs of ELL students centered on helping interns understand that formal and informal assessment is embedded in the daily life of the classroom. Participants shared ways to facilitate ELL students' processing of information and approaches they encouraged their interns to use. These included: (a) building experiences from concrete to abstract, color coding, visual aids, and rubrics; and (b) giving opportunities for oral expression, such as, time to talk and share with others students, time to be in cooperative groups, and time to work one-on-one with a teacher.

Cooperating teachers were adamant about the need for interns to understand the big picture of what they would be teaching and to design their lessons accordingly. One teacher used the metaphor of a pyramid to model how teachers design essential learning or the "pieces you know you want all of them to get." In these discussions, participants understood the connections between equity and teacher expectations. They emphasized that the essential content must be represented to the pupils with high expectations that all students will learn it. For example, a cooperating teacher described successes using unit organizers that present essential ideas to students:

We expect everyone to do the work and then we provide all kinds of other opportunities to make sure they are successful and that they can learn the work . . . it has made our ESL kids feel so much better about being in class and so much more excited about participating.

Lastly, participants emphasized those practices that infused language into their classrooms, immersed students in language, and encouraged students to pursue what they wanted to learn. These included providing free access to a wide range of reading books; labeling items in the classroom; taking time to discuss and write words and make note of their origins and relationships to words in different languages; and teaching language and content together by providing terminology both orally and visually. These examples of successful practices illuminate ways the participants defined their roles as mediators/facilitators of content learning, language models for students, and as facilitators of English language acquisition.

Teachers as Leaders and Advocates for ELL Students

The data also provided evidence of leadership and advocacy roles assumed by cooperating teachers. Participants spoke with authority and conviction on issues of pedagogy, classroom management strategies, curricular adaptations for ELL students, philosophies regarding transitioning ELL students into the mainstream, and advocacy work. Cooperating teachers provided testimonials related to their reverence for their profession and love of students. They shared examples of their convictions that teachers should take opportunities to connect to their students. One comment captured this notion, "Two years ago a Hispanic girl came up to me and said 'I love it when you wear jeans,' and from then on, I wore jeans ... once in a while just for Erika, because Erika likes that."

Participants also shared how they assumed leadership in mentoring interns to work with ELL students. One cooperating teacher described how she interacted with an intern:

I said, 'you want to try this tomorrow? This is what I would do, this is my objective, this is how, try it!' . . . [intern's response was]—'Well I don't know?' 'If you make a mistake, you make a mistake, I'll be there.' So I think it's very important to get them in with the kids and working as soon as possible."

The other realm of teacher leadership is advocacy. The advocacy initiatives participants described related to smoothing the transition of ELL students to the mainstream and seeking advice and support of the ESL teacher. One participant made a point of regularly having lunch with the ESL teacher. Others sought resources and materials that would facilitate ELL student learning. Cooperating teachers emphasized these practices for their interns within the context of creating a meaningful and rich learning environment for ELL students.

Recommendations and Outcomes

Participants offered recommendations for development of a web-based support system. To assist them in their work with ELL students and in mentoring interns to meet the needs of these students, they suggested that stories illustrative of successes with ELL students be posted. They also recommended that suggestions for communicating with ELL students' parents and for conducting parent-teacher conferences be available. Cooperating teachers expressed the need for information about different cultures, including information on educational systems in different countries and community resources that could support them in their cross-cultural work with ELL students and parents.

The teachers recommended that the interactive portion of the site provide opportunities to post questions and concerns and allow for discussion amongst cooperating teachers, interns, and university faculty. A major outcome of this study is that a web site inclusive of the aforementioned recommendations is currently under development. Furthermore, project staff are planning a professional development institute for cooperating teachers based on the results of this study.

Implications for Teacher Educators

We learned that our cooperating teachers were confident in their work and understood their roles in teaching language and content and in organizing their classroom for productive learning. A consistent focus among participants centered on how they made their classrooms places that provided meaningful and connected experiences for their pupils.

The comments of our cooperating teachers regarding their roles in teaching and mentoring to meet the needs of ELL students focused on understanding students as opposed to lesson planning and use of certain strategies. They underscored the need to prepare interns to assess student needs to better teach content, rather than to use different strategies. They stressed the importance of spending time to learn about students, before assuming that a particular lesson or strategy should be used.

The comments of our cooperating teachers also focused on how to connect interns to pupils so they would feel comfortable trusting them to teach the curriculum. If we could give this message their voice we think it might say . . . *"Teaching is hard work; we must constantly reinvent it and ourselves in the process of adapting content to the needs of our pupils."* In essence they were saying—*"You [university teacher educators] are not preparing the teacher candidate for what they will be expected to do on the job."*

Given this study, we see opportunities to provide support for mainstream teachers in their teaching of ELL students. University and school-based teachers educators can through meaningful dialogue begin to shape appropriate experiences for the teacher candidate that stress assessment of learner needs and the development of plans and teaching strategies that match and align with those needs. Voices of the school-based teacher educator must be included as we prepare new professionals to reach and teach linguistically and culturally diverse students.

REFERENCES

Adger, C.T., & Clair, N. (1999). *Professional Development for Implementing Standards in Culturally Diverse Schools.* Paper presented at an invitational conference sponsored by the National Educational Research Policy and Priorities Board, the Office of Educational Research and Improvement and the Office of Bilingual Education and Minority Languages Affairs, Washington, D.C.

Carrasquillo, A.L., & Rodriguez, V. (1996). *Language Minority Students in the Mainstream Classroom.* Bristol, PA: Multilingual Matters Ltd.

Erickson, F. (1986). Qualitative methods in research on teaching. In M. C. Wittrock (Ed.), *Handbook of Research on Teaching* (pp. 119–161). New York: Macmillan.

Flores, J.G., & Alonso, C.G. (1995). Using focus groups in educational research. *Evaluation Review, 19* (1), 84–101.

Glaser, B. G., & Strauss, L.L. (1967). *The Discovery of Grounded Theory: Strategies for Qualitative Research.* Chicago: Aldine.

Glickman, C.D., & Bey, T.M. (1990). Supervision. In W. Robert Houston (Ed.), *Handbook of Research on Teacher Education* (pp. 549–568). New York: Macmillan.

Guyton, E., & McIntyre, J.D. (1990). Student teaching and school experiences. In W. Robert Houston (Ed.), *Handbook of Research on Teacher Education* (pp. 514-534). New York: Macmillan.

Hamayan, E.V. (1990). Preparing Mainstream Teachers to Teach Potentially English Proficient Students. In *Proceedings of the First Research Symposium on Limited English Proficient Students' Issues* (pp. 1–21). Washington, D.C.: Office of Bilingual Education and Minority Languages Affairs.

Knowles, G.J., and Cole, A.L. (1996). Developing Practice Through Field Experiences. In F. B. Murray, (Ed.), *The Teacher Educator's Handbook: Building a Knowledge Base for the Preparation of Teachers* (pp. 648–690). San Francisco: Jossey-Bass.

Moll, L.C., & Gonzalez, N. (1997). Teachers as Social Scientists: Learning about Culture from Household Research. In P.M. Hall (Ed.), *Race, Ethnicity, and Multiculturalism: Policy and Practice* (pp. 89–114). New York: Garland.

National Council for the Accreditation of Teacher Education. (2001). *Professional Standards for the Accreditation of Schools, Colleges, and Departments of Education.* Author: Washington, D.C.

Peredo, M.W. (1999). *Directions in Professional Development.* Washington, D.C.: National Clearinghouse for Bilingual Education.

Ruiz-de-Velasco, J., & Fix, M. (2000). *Overlooked and Underserved: Immigrant Students in U.S. Secondary Schools.* Washington, D.C: The Urban Institute.

Villegas, A.M. & Lucas, T. (2002). Preparing Culturally Responsive Teachers: Rethinking the Curriculum. *Journal of Teacher Education, 53*(1), 20–32.

Successful Reading Achievement in "Beat the Odds" Schools[1]

8.

Martha A. Adler

Martha A. Adler is an Assistant Professor in Reading and Language Arts at the University of Michigan-Dearborn and, previously, a research associate with the Center for the Improvement of Early Reading Achievement (CIERA), the University of Michigan-Ann Arbor. Her research focuses on the relationship between policy and practice within early literacy instruction.

ABSTRACT

This chapter presents the findings of a cross-case analysis of six "beat the odds" elementary schools, selected from respondents to a national survey of high-poverty, high-performing schools identified through the examination of local and state reading scores over a three-year period (1996–1998) and with 50 percent or more students eligible for free/reduced lunch. Each of these schools has evidence of able and stable leadership at the school level and competent instruction at the classroom level. They also have systematic schoolwide arrangements to provide continuous support for struggling readers. The fact that both sound classroom instruction and systematic arrangements are necessary to produce unusually high reading performances for nearly all students is a critical understanding for current and future educators. While sound classroom instruction is a necessary foundation, it is insufficient for high-poverty schools without the presence of schoolwide mechanisms that can leverage the effects of classroom instruction.

Objectives

A considerable amount of information has been amassed regarding schools that have effected change through schoolwide programming, such as has occurred under Title I implementation (USDOE, 1998a); however, information on how high-poverty, high-performing schools achieve their success specific to their early reading programs and what distinguishes them from their low-performing counterparts is not immediately clear. If we are serious about improving the quality of reading instruction and preparing educators to achieve success with all children in early reading achievement in our nation's schools, it is critical that we understand what is working well. This study investigates early reading programs in high-poverty, high-performing schools and asks two key questions: What characteristics do high-poverty, high-performing schools share that distinguish them from their low-achieving counterparts? And, how do these schools plan, organize, and implement their successful early reading programs within their available resources?

Theoretical Framework

BACKGROUND OF THE PROBLEM

The concern for low-performing, high-poverty public elementary schools and early reading achievement have become a primary focus of recent educational reform efforts. Empirical data on schools that beat the odds with regard to early reading achievement are scarce. Indeed, the literature on early reading has historically focused on issues of classroom instruction. Many studies represent comparisons of particular instructional methodologies applied to classrooms. The First-Grade Studies (Bond & Dykstra, 1967) and their reinterpretation three decades later (see Special Edition of Reading Research Quarterly, 1997) provide considerable insight into the dilemmas of early reading. However, neither studies of reading methods, nor other studies of reading (see for example Pearson , Barr, Kamil & Mosenthal, 1984; Barr, Kamil, Mosenthal & Pearson, 1991; and Hiebert & Raphael, 1998 for reviews), provide insights into the programmatic mechanisms that allow some schools, especially high poverty schools, to obtain consistently good performance for their early readers.

The perception that public schools are not successful in teaching poor children to read fluently and with comprehension by the fourth grade is not unfounded. High poverty schools continue to struggle with reading improvement. In 1998, the U.S. Department of Education completed its third wave of assessments (USDOE, 1999), the National Assessment of Education Progress (NAEP), including measures of reading achievement at grade 4. For the first time, NAEP data allow comparisons between students who are eligible for free/reduced lunch and those who are not. These data provided national-level information on just how well early reading programs were performing. While there was limited good news in these NAEP data, they also revealed long-standing and unacceptably large differences in reading performance related to student poverty levels. For example, at grade four, 59 percent of students eligible for free/reduced lunch scored below the "basic" achievement standard set by NAEP compared to only 27 percent of students who were not eligible. If the achievement criterion is raised to "proficient," then 87 percent of grade four students who were eligible for free/reduced lunch fell below their ineligible peers. This pattern also persists in more recent NAEP data; they show a widening gap in achievement levels. Early reading programs are not working adequately for children in poverty. If our educational system is to serve our nation's students equitably, these enormous differences simply must be reduced.

Students placed at risk by poverty are not evenly distributed among our nation's school districts, nor are they evenly distributed between schools within districts. And, as the NAEP data (and data from other sources, such as state- and nationally-standardized achievement data) imply, average reading performance for a school tends to decrease as the proportion of students eligible for free/reduced lunch increases. Hence, the statistical expectation for reading performance in high-poverty schools is relatively low. However, these results do not reflect all high poverty schools. There are high-poverty schools that "beat the odds," where very large proportions of students in the school perform at or above the state average on early reading measures. Students in these schools, in contrast to other high-poverty schools, are able to learn to read fluently and with comprehension by the end of the primary grades. And they do so while operating with similarly high percentages of students eligible for free/reduced lunch, similarly high percentages of student mobility rates, similar curriculum frameworks, and similar per pupil expenditures.

LITERATURE REVIEW

It was perhaps not until the 1960s with the war on poverty declared that we began as a nation to pay attention to the large numbers of public school children struggling with reading achievement. The response to the problem was swift and dramatic from both the public and private sectors. Title I of the Elementary and Secondary Education Act was born as an instrument of change, Title IV of the Civil Rights Act led to the desegregation of our nation's schools, and the First Grade Studies (Bond & Dykstra, 1967) were commissioned. Individuals like Comer (1997) led the way to what was to become one of many school improvement models and Edmonds (1979) was to influence the effective schools movement with his simple, yet to-the-core and oft-repeated, message that all children can learn. The extensive body of research that has been developing for at least four decades on both effective reading instruction and effective schools has built a foundation upon which no child should be left behind because of reading failure. The evidence is clear and compelling: children who do not learn to read and comprehend fluently and independently by the end of the early grades will have few opportunities to catch up and virtually no chance to surpass their peers who are reading on grade level by the end of the third grade. Yet, the problem persists in our nation's schools. For poor, language-minority, and/or dialect-speaking children growing up in urban environments and attending low-performing schools the odds of successful early reading achievement are not in their favor (Snow, Burns & Griffin, 1998).

Within the voluminous literature on early reading, the vast majority is focused on instructional issues in classrooms (Adams, 1990; Allington & McGill-Franzen, 1993; Bond & Dykstra, 1967; Chall, 1967; Chall, 1999; Hiebert, Pearson, Taylor, Richardson, & Paris, 1998; Hiebert & Raphael, 1998; Hiebert & Taylor, 1994; Kamil, Mosenthal, Pearson, & Barr, 2000; Institute of Child Health and Human Development, 2000; Snow, Burns & Griffin, 1998). The recent publications of the National Research Council's (Snow et al., 1998) review of this literature and the Report of National Reading Panel (Institute of Child Health and Human Development, 2000) provide the most comprehensive overview to date on what we know as a field about teaching children to read. Effective and powerful instruction from teachers knowledgeable in the reading process is the key to successful early reading achievement for all children, regardless of socio-economic status and/or home language. While not all children enter public school with the same level of preparedness, the excellent balanced instruction that provides all children opportunities to (a) master concepts of print, the alphabetic principle, word recognition skills, phonemic awareness, (b) engage and sustain an interest in reading, with a wide range of materials with fluency and comprehension, and (c) begin where the child is developmentally continues to be the major preventative against reading failure (Adams, 1990; Hiebert et al., 1998; Institute of Child Health and Human Development, 2000; Snow et al., 1998).

However, it takes more than individual teachers and solid research-based curriculum and materials to achieve success for every child in the early grades, particularly for children who are at risk of not achieving academic excellence because of poverty and/or attendance at high-poverty, urban schools (Snow et al., 1998). Poverty alone does not serve as a predictor of either reading difficulties nor as a barrier to achievement, but it does have significant impact on learners if they are concentrated in high numbers in any one school. Schoolwide effects matter; and while we have no control over whether or not a child is poor or attends an urban school, we do have control over the quality of the schools children attend and the level of reading instruction those schools provide. There is no doubt from the research conducted in the past thirty years, that we can teach children to read (Institute of Child Health and Human Development, 2000; Snow et al., 1998) and that schools can make a difference (Darling-Hammond, 1997; Rossi & Stringfield, 1997; Stringfield, 1994).

Multiple efforts to recognize high-poverty, high-performing schools are evidence that there is an underlying trust in the fact that schools with high concentrations of poor children can achieve reading success. The IAS Title I Distinguished Schools program sponsored by the United States Department of Education (USDOE) has established an impressive list of successful schoolwide programs for a number of years. Investigations of these high performing Title I schools (Billig, 1998; Lein, Johnson & Ragland, 1997), the White House call to identify and work with "turn around" schools (USDOE, 1998a), the publication of the Idea Book for implementing schoolwide Title I programs (USDOE, 1998b); and the current calls to "leave no child behind" continue the efforts to improve the quality of education for our nation's poor. Yet, not much is known about how these high-poverty, high-performing schools achieve early reading success or what distinguishes them from their low-performing counterparts.

One exception is Hoffman and Rutherford's (1984) review of effective reading programs from the 1970s using an "outlier" paradigm where

> the identification and study of a school or set of schools which have been highly successful in terms of their effects on pupil achievement where extra-institutional factors would predict patterns of failure. Common characteristics of effective schools as revealed by the studies are organized around the dimensions of program characteristics, leadership behaviors, and psychological conditions (p. 79).

These studies varied widely in their scope and focus; however, findings from individual studies that point to the relevance of schoolwide programming include: a strong curriculum; high expectations with a strong focus on improving reading achievement; a system of accountability and careful evaluation of student progress; strong instructional leadership; breadth of materials; communication of ideas across teachers; time spent in reading instruction as well as the time to develop and achieve schoolwide success.

More recent efforts to understand and effect positive improvement for schools with children designated at risk because of poverty have generally focused on (a) specific programs and/or projects (Slavin, Karweit, & Madden, 1989; Shields, Knapp, & Wechsler, 1995; Stringfield, Millsap, & Herman, 1997), (b) the establishment and widespread acceptance of compensatory programs (Allington, 1993; Billig, 1998; Lein, Johnson & Ragland, 1997), and (c) the investigations of schools as highly reliable organizations (e.g., Stringfield, 1994). While these various studies looked at a range of schools, each identified similar attributes that have schoolwide implications for effective reading achievement, such as (a) quality curriculum and classroom instruction (Allington & McGill-Franzen, 1993; Quellmalz, Shields, and Knapp, 1995; Shields et al., 1995), (b) collaboration, community building and professional development (Frazee, 1996), (c) support systems outside schools and research-based reading/language arts content (George, Grissom & Just, 1996), (d) curriculum and assessment alignment (Rossi & Stringfield, 1997), (e) clear and agreed-upon goals and objectives at national, state, and school levels (Rossi & Stringfield, 1997), (f) high expectations (Edmonds, 1979; Frazee, 1996), (g) early interventions and strategies for struggling readers (Legters & McDill, 1994), and (f) leadership and commitment (George, Grissom & Just, 1996). However, information limited to early reading instruction for high-poverty schools is not easily teased out of these effective schoolwide studies. Often results are combined for both elementary and secondary schools with high and low poverty populations; and coverage of instruction in more than one core academic area (e.g., reading and math) diminishes the amount of information available in early reading.

Perhaps more important than citing the names of programs that have proven effective in teaching children who fall at the bottom of the 25th percentile in reading success is to cite what the research has revealed about programmatic and organizational aspects of teaching children who do not learn to read at the same success rates as their peers. Since availability of programs, commitment from administrators, funding, and training of teachers influence programs that eventually become adopted by schools, it makes more sense to obtain a deep understanding of what it is that promotes successful reading achievement so that individual schools can become better consumers of programs available to them. Reasons for looking at early reading instruction specifically from an organizational and programmatic perspective are compelling. Allington (1993) describes two systems of education, one as it existed during the period prior to the implementation of federal compensatory and categorical programs and the second as it exists as these programs have developed and been implemented since their introduction. He argues that well-intended programs led to the fracturing of early reading instruction where classroom teachers no longer saw themselves in control of teaching reading to all of their children. Children identified as eligible for these programs were provided for in pull-out situations, leaving the potential for serious gaps in their instruction. However, with the reauthorization and restructuring of Title I in 1994, the potential for these programs to be instrumental in mending the fractures created by past programming is realized. In fact we see evidence of this in the high-poverty, high-performing schools we, and others, have investigated.

A handful of recent studies include descriptions of some high-poverty high-performing schools (Adler, 2002; Adler & Fisher, 2001 & 1999; Briggs & Thomas, 1997; Fisher, Adler, Noorani, & Tesnar, 1998; Foertsch, 1997, 1998; Miles & Darling-Hammond, 1997; Taylor, Peterson, Cappello, Clark, & Halvorson, 1998; Taylor, Pearson, Clark, & Walpole, 1999; Pearson, Dewitz, Danridge, & Breaux, 1998). There are large differences among these studies in how high-poverty is defined and in the breadth of subject matter examined. In spite of these differences, there appears to be some convergence in their findings. These emerging studies of early reading in high-poverty, high-performing schools provide solid support for the significance of both sound classroom instruction and systematic schoolwide arrangements in order to produce unusually high reading performances for nearly all students. These findings reflect many of the features highlighted in the research on effective schools and effective reading instruction.

Methods

This qualitative study relied primarily on descriptive case study methodology and analysis (Guba & Lincoln, 1981; Dexter, 1970; Gorden, 1969; Mertens, 1998; Skate, 1995; Yin, 1984). Data were collected and analyzed in five stages from April 1998 to April 2000.

In the first stage, a sample of schools that "beat the odds" were identified and invited to participate in a survey of early literacy programs. Schools in the sample met two criteria: (a) at least 50% of students eligible for free or reduced lunch, and (b) at least 50% of students achieving satisfactory or proficient reading levels on standardized reading assessments for a three-year consecutive period. The primary source for these schools was the list of Title I Distinguished Schools (1995–1998) and selected state lists of high performance schools (1995–1998). This process resulted in the identification of 430 schools nationwide, who were then invited to participate in the Center for the Improvement of Early Reading Achievement (CIERA) Survey (1998) on early reading programs.

In the second stage, the 140 schools in 39 states who responded to both the principal and teacher versions of the CIERA Survey of Early Literacy Programs in High Performing Schools (1998) were screened for possible selection as case studies. A network of informants who could provide further information on particular schools from national, state, and local perspectives was identified. We examined data on state assessment practices and school participation rates in state testing (where available). Consideration was also given to demographic characteristics, such as geographical region of the country, urban versus rural populations, school size, range of grade levels, and presence of language minority and bilingual students.

In the third phase, case studies were conducted in six schools in three states (California, Michigan, and Texas). Schools selected for case study development were invited to participate through initial telephone contact with the principal. Subsequent contact with the school and scheduling of interviews and classroom visits was left to the school's principal and staff. Data obtained for each school included (a) fifty-two "elite" interviews (Guba & Lincoln, 1981; Dexter, 1970) of approximately 45 minutes to an hour; interviewees included school principals, primary classroom and early reading teachers; (b) classroom observations of approximately 10 to 12 hours per school in classrooms of both teachers interviewed and those not; (c) field and journal notes of observations and informal conversations with administrators, teaching staff and other personnel (e.g., aides, librarians, and custodial staff); (d) artifacts from the early reading programs, and (e) relevant school, district, and state documents for each site (e.g. curriculum and standards information, achievement data, and per pupil expenditures, available in print format and from state websites). Throughout the study, the data collection process was dynamic in that data were continually reviewed and annotated prior to each subsequent school visit for theoretical interpretations, methodological alterations and for clarity of events observed and/or conversations held (Gorden, 1969).

For the fourth stage of the study invitations to low-performing, high-poverty schools were extended in an effort to develop one to two comparison case studies. None of the schools responded; therefore, we were unable to replicate the study with low-achieving schools. Thus, we have moved forward with the final stage, the cross case analysis reported here in this paper.

Data Source

CASE STUDY SCHOOLS

Each of the six schools were selected from respondents to the CIERA survey of high-poverty, high-performing schools that were identified through the examination of local and state reading scores over a three-year period (1996-1998) for schools with populations of 50 percent or more students eligible for free/reduced lunch. From this group six schools in six districts in Michigan, Texas, and California were selected for further investigation. Tables 1 and 2 provide comparison data for the six schools. School populations eligible for free and reduced lunch ranged from 50 to 89 percent and all reported 20 to 40 percent mobility rates. All schools sustained their reading achievement for at least two consecutive years with 50 percent or more of their students achieving at or above the satisfactory level for their respective state reading/language arts assessments by the fourth grade.

Limited English proficient enrollments ranged from 0–4 percent in half the schools to 35–37 percent in other half, with Spanish being the dominant second language. Grade levels ranged from pre-kindergarten to fifth grade. School enrollments range from 412–829. All of the schools were located in urban or urban fringe areas. One school was approximately thirty minutes from the Rio Grande River and had many students with close ties to families in Mexico.

TABLE 1						
1997–1998 Demographic Data						
School	White	Black	Hispanic	Asian/ Pacific	Native America	Bilingual/ LEP
MI 1	67%	31%	1%	<1%	0	0
MI 2	8%	91%	<1%	0	0	0
TX 3	5%	<1%	95%	0	0	37%
TX 4	27%	31%	36%	6%	0	4%
CA 5	48%	10%	37%	3%	1%	35%
CA 6	18%	25%	49%	8%	<1%	36%

TABLE 2 1997–1998 School Data						
School	Per Pupil $	FRL	Enrollment	Grades	Bilingual Instruction	Location
MI 1	$4002	86%	412	K–5	None	Urban Fringe of a large city
MI 2	$4983	50%	464	Pre K–5	None	Urban
TX 3	$4043	71%	497	Pre K–5	Bilingual Programs	Urban Fringe of mid-size city
TX 4	$4114	84%	514	Pre K–5	None	Urban
CA 5	$4228	89%	829	K–5	Bilingual Programs	Urban Fringe of a large city
CA 6	$4022	71%	755	K–5 Year-round	Bilingual Programs	Urban

Per pupil funding was similar for all these schools, with the lowest at $4,002 and the highest at $4,983. None of these per pupil expenditures was significantly different for other schools in the same districts.

Results and Conclusions

For these six schools, we identified systematic school-wide characteristics of their early reading programs that appear to set these schools apart. As is the case for public education, each of the six schools had to deal with the dynamics of district and state issues on a daily basis. For example, at the time of the study, the California schools with their high percentages of Spanish speaking children were dealing with both the recently passed State Proposition 227, which essentially required dismantling bilingual instruction and the introduction of a new state assessment instrument (Stanford IX). For the Michigan schools, one district had just purchased a new basal series that the teachers found impractical for their at-risk students who needed more language and emergent reading skills development; another Michigan school was dealing with the imminent take over of its district by the state's governor. The Texas schools had the increasing pressure to perform well on the Texas Assessment of Academic Skills (TAAS). Key findings are grouped under three headings: key elements of school operation, key elements of early reading program, and implications for resource allocation. Each is discussed below.

KEY ELEMENTS OF SCHOOL OPERATION

Leadership

It should come as no surprise that each of the six schools have able and stable leadership at the school level; however, it is important to note that this leadership is of two types, administrative and instructional. Administrative leadership in all of the schools was carried out by the primary building principal. In three schools there are two administrators per building,[2] one always taking on the primary administrative role. In this administrative position, principals provides the bridge between school and district, acting as the broker for the school in obtaining district resources, overseeing key elements of school operations, such as budget allocations and staffing, supporting professional development opportunities for staff, and promoting shared decision making and collaboration among staff.

The instructional leadership evident in all the schools is not always provided by the same individuals. In two of the schools, a core of knowledgeable teachers provides support for staff on early reading instruction. In another, the Title I support and reading resource teacher provides leadership. One school looks to its district's reading coordinator for instructional guidance and training, and building administrators provide the leadership and support in two other schools.

A Core of Experienced and Knowledgeable Teachers

In each of the schools a core of teachers provide years of experience in the early grades. In all of the schools, new teachers are being hired as enrollments increase, class sizes decrease (e.g., as in California), and as many of the more experienced teachers retired. However, in each of these schools, the experienced teachers provide support for new staff, ranging form formal arrangements such as the California mentoring program that one school implements to informal pairings of first time teachers with their senior peers. Teachers also provide mentoring for one another; senior staff readily accept information on instruction and/or strategies from others, even those with fewer years in the classroom. Many teachers also hold advanced degrees in areas such as reading, early childhood, and special education.

Shared Responsibility and Focus on Early Reading Achievement

Each of these schools can be described as taking the responsibility for student success very seriously. These are what we like to call blameless schools. When a child is not achieving, they do not look for excuses, but rather they seek solutions. Consequently, they work together, as is evidenced by the variety of mechanisms in place, such as safety nets (Table 3) implemented toward achieving academic success for all their students. The schools have a shared focus on early reading, even those working with older children. All staff are willing to do what it takes to help their students achieve success. Many work beyond the school day and/or school year providing one-on-one and/or small group tutoring for struggling readers. Teachers also make use of what time they have during the day for tutoring or for curriculum and instructional planning. In many cases, this extra time is not reimbursed; only a few of the schools provided hourly pay for after school tutoring.

Ongoing Professional Development

Professional development is valued and expected at all the schools. Ongoing training in reading instruction varies from school to school and seems to reflect the instructional leadership at each of the schools with some training occurring on site, at the district, and/or at the state levels. Many teachers

TABLE 3
Examples of Safety Nets for Struggling Readers

During School Day	Before/After School	Extended Year
One on One	One on One	Small group
Teachers tutor	Teachers tutor	Summer School
Small Group	Small Group	Inter-session
In-class	Extended day program	Extended school year
Whole Class		

hold or are pursuing advanced degrees and participate in state and national professional conferences. It was also not uncommon to find that many of the teachers in the study were presenters at district, state and/or national conferences.

Collaboration/Team Approach to Planning

School wide collaboration in all of these schools is complex and carried out in a variety of ways. What is most significant about this collaboration is that it goes across grades (vertical) as well as within grades (horizontal). There are any number of arrangements at each of these schools. For example, all of the schools have some form of a school-based committee. While the title of this group varies from school to school, the roles are very similar. Such a committee is generally composed of grade level representatives, resource teachers, and an administrator, with their primary role as support for instructional programming. Thus, proposals, such as one requesting a shift in the number of paraprofessionals from the upper grades to increase their number at the lower grades in order to provide more small group reading instruction to first graders, are submitted; reviewed; and subsequently acted on. Other structures within each of these schools include both within grade and across grade level committees that meet on a regular basis.

Grade level meetings occur on a weekly or bi-weekly basis in each of the schools. These meetings provide opportunities for same grade teachers to collaborate on curriculum, instructional strategies, and, most importantly, on individual children. Teachers rely on one another for assistance with their struggling readers, and it is not uncommon for individual children to be brought up in these meetings.

Across grade level meetings occur less frequently, usually 2–4 times a year. During these meetings teachers have opportunities to share specific grade level goals and curriculum. Because of these across grade level structures, staff have very clear expectations of what children coming into their grade level will have been taught as well as what the grade level above them expects children to have learned.

KEY ELEMENTS OF EARLY READING PROGRAM

Flexible and Dynamic Student Grouping

In all of the early reading programs grouping for reading instruction is varied within a classroom. Teachers move from whole group to small group and one-on-one instruction throughout their reading and language arts instruction. Small groups are used for specific skills instruction. Children do not remain in a particular group for the entire year. Membership of any these small groups may only last for a few weeks for an individual child. When needed, one-on-one tutoring is provided at all the schools. In some cases, this is very formal, as is the case with schools that have Reading Recovery programs. In others, it is informal, perhaps a teacher working one-on-one with a student while the rest of the class in involved with small-group or independent work. In almost all the schools, these groups occur within the classroom; push-in dominates over pull-out groupings.

Ongoing Student Assessment for Instruction

All of the teachers have systems for assessing students' instructional needs. These range from daily running records and checking students' knowledge of high frequency words to published instruments, such as the "Texas Reading Inventory" or basal assessment instruments. Teachers are very artic- ulate about their students' individual instructional needs and keep ongoing records that they refer to for lesson planning and instructional decisions.

Safety Nets for Struggling Readers

Schoolwide mechanisms are in place to support struggling readers, espe- cially in grades 1 through 3. Table 3 provides a sampling of the types of pro- grams that individual schools have in place for their struggling readers. These programs occur as part of the regular school day though a variety of formats. In some schools instructional support relies on commercial pro- grams, such as "Project Read" or "Reading Recovery" and is formally scheduled into the daily routine. Many schools provide tutoring during the day for their students, during a teacher's prep or lunch time. All of the schools have some extended day tutoring, which occurs before or after school. Some schools use before and after school care programs to provide one-on-one tutoring. Two of the schools have formal extended day programs during second semester and all of the schools provide additional support during the summer. Finally, some schools structure their students for long- term support, such as the 3rd grade academy at one California school. This program places struggling readers together in order to get them caught up before the transition back into the regular classrooms by the 4th grade.

Multiple Approaches to Reading Instruction

Primary teachers in all six schools are responsible for reading instruction to all their students in their classrooms, spending on average two hours a day in reading and language arts instruction. Reading and language arts include strong instruction in both reading and writing. Reading instruction is balanced, using both whole language and phonics-based models. Teachers do not rely on one method or philosophy for teaching their students to read; with the on-going assessment teachers practice, instruction is responsive to student needs. While teachers speak of constantly learning about teaching reading, they do not quickly change totally what they do instructionally. They constantly seek solutions to their students' struggles and select what works and discard what does not. Thus, in all of these classrooms, materials and instruction are eclectic, yet balanced (i.e., skills based as well as literature based). In addition, writing (such as journaling or writer's workshops) occurs daily in these classrooms.

IMPLICATIONS FOR RESOURCE ALLOCATION

Funding

Per pupil funding in each of these schools (Table 2) is not significantly different from comparable schools within their districts. Many of the schools are in high-poverty districts and thus receive similar funds, such as Title I monies. In fact, Title I funds seem to support many of the safety nets that schools have in place. Most of school funding is dependent upon federal, state, and local funding. However, one school relies on bilingual and migrant funding to support their bilingual students. Two other schools receive some additional funding from two national programs (Comer and Core Knowledge respectively); however, none of the funding from these programs goes directly to instruction or reading program implementation. In addition, schools take proactive stances toward allocating their funds. They are continually in problem solving modes and ready to make use of funds when they become available. For example, one school reported that it is common knowledge that every spring, the district finds extra money. Rather than wait for the announcement, they are ready with their proposal as soon as it appears, thus optimizing their chances at obtaining the extra funding.

Programmatic Decisions

All of the schools reported that decisions on implementation of reading programs are made at the school level. As previously mentioned, all of the schools have various committees in place that deal specifically with instructional and programmatic decisions. These groups are empowered to act on their decisions. In some cases, teachers have had to go to their board for approval, but in most cases implementation for reading program changes occur at the school level. It is also the case that administrators in each of these schools control staffing as well.

Time

Looking at these programs over time (i.e. 5–10 years), it is obvious that they have had the time to grow. None of these schools became successful over night. Each school's history reflects periods of experimentation. In addition, these histories reveal far more that just reading programming. Schools have had to deal with non-productive school climates, restructuring as a result of district growth, and the various political and educational changes over time. Their respective histories show the dynamic natures of these schools.

Time provides another resource to these schools in how it is allocated for instruction and planning both across the school year and from day to day. These schools have had to be very creative in order to put many of their programs, particularly the safety nets into place.

CONCLUSIONS

The field needs more elaborated models that account for both the effects of classroom instruction and the effects of specific schoolwide mechanisms. We need additional studies to determine whether the leveraging effect of schoolwide mechanisms consistently increases with increasing levels of school poverty. Greater understanding of this dynamic would allow more effective allocation of resources to support high-poverty schools.

However, as expected from previous research (Hoffman & Rutherford, 1984; USDOE, 1998a), this study shows that these schools have evidence of able and stable leadership at the school level and a core of experienced, knowledgeable and dedicated teachers in the early grades. In addition, each of the schools has put specific schoolwide mechanisms in place to support struggling readers, especially in grades 1 through 3. The schools also have well-developed procedures for working with young students who transferred into the school either at the beginning of or during, the school year. These mechanisms invariably require some kind of within-grade and across-grade level communication about the status of struggling readers on a regular basis. While these mechanisms fulfill common functions from school to school, the mechanisms themselves appeared to be idiosyncratic. It was also clear that these schools did not acquire their high-performance status quickly, rather they had undergone a series of developmental stages or phases. In short, although these high-performing high-poverty schools had competent instruction at the classroom level, they also had systematic school-wide arrangements to provide continuous support for struggling readers. It appears that both sound classroom instruction and systematic school-wide arrangements are necessary to produce unusually high reading performances for nearly all students. Sound classroom instruction, as one would expect, appears to be a necessary foundation but the presence of school-wide mechanisms appears to leverage the effects of good classroom instruction. Furthermore, leverage appears to be stronger as the level of poverty in the school increases.

Implications for Teachers and Teacher Educators

These findings have strong implications for national and local efforts to improve reading achievement in high-poverty schools. Each of the cases in this study offers educators practical examples of how high-performing, high-poverty schools create and sustain their effects on early reading performance. Everyone needs to be knowledgeable, including current and future educators. Teacher educators can enhance the knowledge base of their students by providing them with both the tools essential for teaching reading and the information regarding what works in existing schools with children at risk for academic achievement because of poverty.

All to often in teacher-preparation literacy courses, we limit our course material to instruction and curriculum at the classroom level. Pre-service teachers need to understand literacy instruction from a school perspective as well. We can better prepare our future teachers if we provide our students with base knowledge that includes an understanding of how schoolwide approaches to literacy achievement are vital to the achievement of individual students, particularly those at risk because of poverty.

Teachers currently working with high-poverty populations or struggling to attain high reading achievement for all their children can benefit from the knowledge that these schools provide. An examination of "beat the odds" schools provides educators, struggling with some of the same issues that these schools deal with, ideas for discussion and self-assessment.

We believe that these issues have implications for the ultimate effectiveness of efforts to facilitate low-performing schools success in reading achievement success for at risk students. We argue that until we develop an understanding of what successful schools have done with their early reading programs in a way that takes into account both schoolwide and classroom planning within the context of early reading, we risk not having the whole story before us.

REFERENCES

Adams, J. J. (1990). *Beginning to Read: Thinking and Learning about Print.* Cambridge, MA: MIT Press.

Adler, M.A. (2002). Serna Elementary School. In B. M. Taylor & P. D. Pearson (Eds.), *Effective Early Reading Classrooms, Programs, and Schools* (pp. 237–259). Mahwah, NJ: Erlbaum.

Adler, M. A., & Fisher, C.W. (1999, December). *A Cross Case Analysis of Successful Early Reading Programs in High Poverty, High Performing Schools.* Paper Presented at the 49th Annual National Reading Conference Meeting, Orlando, FL.

Adler, M.A., & Fisher, C.W. (2001). Early Reading Programs in High Poverty Schools: A Case of Beating the Odds. *Reading Teacher, 54*(67), 616–619.

Allington, R.L. (1993). *Reducing the Risk: Integrated Language Arts in Restructured Elementary Schools.* Report Series 1.8. Albany, NY: National Research Center on Literature Teaching and Learning.

Allington, R. L., & McGill-Franzen, A. (1993). Placing Children at Risk: Schools Respond to Reading Problems. In R. Donmoyer & R. Kos (Eds.), *At-Risk Students* (pp. 197–217). Albany, NY: State University of New York Press.

Barr, R., Kamil, M., Mosenthal, P., & Pearson, D. (Eds.) (1991). *Handbook of Research on Reading (Vol. II).* New York: Longman.

Billig, S. H. (1998). Implementation of Title 1 of the Improving America's Schools Act: A 1997–1998 Update. *Journal of Education for Students at Risk, 3*(3), 209–222.

Bond, G., & Dykstra, R. (1967). The Cooperative Research Program in First-Grade Reading Instruction. *Reading Research Quarterly, 2*(4), 1–142.

Briggs, K., & Thomas, K. (1997). *Patterns of Success: Successful Pathways to Elementary Literacy in Texas Spotlight Schools.* Austin, TX: Texas Center for Educational Research.

Chall, J. (1967). *Learning to Read: The Great Debate.* NY: McGraw-Hill.

Chall, J.S., (1999). Some Thoughts on Reading Research: Revisiting the First-Grade Studies. *Reading Research Quarterly, 34*(1), 8–10.

CIERA Survey of Early Literacy Programs in High Performing Schools: Principal Survey. (1998). Ann Arbor, MI: CIERA/University of Michigan.

CIERA Survey of Early Literacy Programs in High Performing Schools: Teacher Survey. (1998). Ann Arbor, MI: CIERA/University of Michigan.

Comer, J. P. (1997). *Waiting for a Miracle: Why Schools Can't Solve Our Problems and How We Can.* NY: Dutton.

Darling-Hammond, L. (1997). *The Right to Learn: A Blueprint for Creating Schools that Work.* San Francisco: Jossey-Bass Publishers.

Dexter, L.A. (1970). *Elite and Specialized Interviewing*. Evanston, IL: Northwestern University Press.

Edmonds, R. (1979). Effective schools for the urban poor. *Educational Leadership, 37*(1), 15–24.

Fisher, C. W., Adler, M. A., Noorani, F., & Tesnar, K. (1998, December). *Early Reading Programs in High-Poverty Schools: A Case Study of Beating the Odds*. Paper presented at National Reading Conference, Austin TX.

Fisher, C.W., & Adler, M.A. (1999). *Early Reading Programs in High-Poverty Schools: Emerald Elementary Beats the Odds*. Ann Arbor, MI: CIERA Technical Report #3-009.

Foertsch, M. (1997). *A Study of School Practices, Instruction, and Achievement in District 31 Schools*. Oak Brook, IL: North Central Regional Educational Laboratory.

Foertsch, M. (1998). *Exemplary Reading Programs in Illinois Public Schools*. Oak Brook, IL: North Central Regional Educational Laboratory.

Frazee, B. M. (1996). Hawthorne Elementary School: The University Perspective. *Journal of Education for Students at Risk, (1)*, 25–31.

George, C.A., Grissom, J.B., & Just, A.E. (1996). Stories of Mixed Success: Program Improvement Implementation in Chapter 1 Schools. *Journal of Students Placed at Risk, (1)*, 77–93.

Gorden, R. L. (1969). *Interviewing: Strategy, Techniques and Tactics*. Homewood, IL: Dorsey Press.

Guba. E.G., & Lincoln, &Y. S. (1981). *Effective Evaluation*. SF: Jossey-Bass Publications.

Hiebert, E.H., & Taylor, B.M. (Eds.). (1994). *Getting Reading Right from the Start: Effective Early Literacy Interventions*. Boston: Allyn & Bacon, Inc.

Hiebert, E.H., Raphael, T. (1998). *Early Literacy Instruction*. Fort Worth, TX: Harcourt Brace College Publishers.

Hiebert, E.H., Pearson, P.D., Taylor, B.M., Richardson, V., & Paris, S.G. (1998). *Every Child a Reader: Applying Reading Research in the Classroom*. Ann Arbor, MI: CIERA.

Hoffman, J.W., & Rutherford, W.L. (1984). Effective Reading Programs: A Critical Review of Outlier Studies. *Reading Research Quarterly, 20*(1), 79–92.

Institute of Child Health and Human Development (2000). *Report of the National Reading Panel-Teaching Children to Read: An Evidence-Based Assessment of the Scientific Research Literature on Reading and Its Implications for Reading Instruction* (NIH Publication No. 00-4769). Washington, DC: U.S. Government Printing Office.

Kamil, M.L, Mosenthal, P. B., Pearson, P.D., & Barr, R. (Eds.) (2000). *Handbook of Reading Instruction, (Vol III)*. Mahwah, NJ: Lawrence Erlbaum Associates.

Lein, L., Johnson, J., & Ragland, M. (1997). *Successful Texas School-Wide Programs: Research Study Results.* Austin, TX: The Charles A. Dana Center.

Letgers, N., & McDill, E. L. (1994). Rising to the Challenge: Emerging Strategies for Educating Youth at Risk. In Robert J. Rossi (Ed.), *Schools and Students at Risk: Context and Framework for Positive Change* (pp. 23–47). NY: Teachers College Press.

Mertens, E.M. (1998). *Research Methods in Education and Psychology: Integrating Diversity with Quantitative and Qualitative Approaches.* Thousand Oaks, CA: Sage Publications.

Miles, K., & Darling-Hammond, L. (1997). *Rethinking the Allocation of Teaching Resources: Some Lessons from High-Performing Schools.* University of Pennsylvania: Consortium for Policy Research in Education.

Pearson, D., Barr, R., Kamil, M., & Mosenthal, P. (Eds.) (1984). *Handbook of Research on Reading (Vol. I).* New York: Longman.

Pearson, P. D., Dewitz, P, Danridge, J., & Breaux, G. (1998, December). *Success in Two Inner City and Two Rural Schools: Investigating Locally Developed and Externally Developed Literacy.* Paper presented at National Reading Conference annual conference, Austin, TX.

Quellmalz, E., Shields, P.M., & Knapp, M.S. (1995). *School-Based Reform: Lessons from a National Study: A Guide for School Reform Teams.* Washington, DC: U.S. Department of Education.

Reading Research Quarterly [Special Issue], Volume 32, Number 4. (1997). Newark, DE: International Reading Association.

Rossi, R. J., & Stringfield, S. C. (1997). *Education Reform and Students at Risk.* Washington, D.C.: Office of Educational Research and Improvement.

Shields, P.M., Knapp, M.S., & Wechsler, M.E. (1995). *Improving Schools from the Bottom Up: From Effective Schools to Restructuring: Summary Volume.* Washington, DC: U.S. Department of Education.

Skate, R.E. (1995). *The Art of Case Study Research.* Thousand Oaks, CA: Sage Publications.

Slavin, R. E., Karweit, N. L., & Madden, N. A. (1989). *Effective Programs for Students at Risk.* Boston: Allyn and Bacon.

Snow, C.E., Burns, M.S., & Griffin, P. (Eds.). (1998). *Preventing Reading Difficulties in Children.* Washington, DC: National Research Council.

Stringfield, S. C. (1994). Identifying and addressing organizational barriers to reform. In Robert J. Rossi (Ed.), *Schools and Students at Risk: Context and Framework for Positive Change* (pp. 277–295). NY: Teachers College Press.

Stringfield, S., Millsap, M.A., & Herman, R. (1997). *Special Strategies for Educating Disadvantaged Children: Findings and Policy Implications of a Longitudinal Study.* Washington, DC: U.S. Department of Education.

Taylor, B. M., Peterson, D., Cappello, M, Clark, K, & Halvorson, B. (1998, December). *Examining Effective Practice in the Primary Grades: Overview and Trends Across Case Studies*. Paper presented at National Reading Conference annual conference, Austin, TX.

Taylor, B. M., Pearson, P. D., Clark, K. F., & Walpole, S. (1999). *Beating the Odds in Teaching All Children to Read* (CIERA Report #2-006). Ann Arbor: MI: CIERA/University of Michigan.

Taylor, B., Walpole, S. (1998, December). *School Factors Contributing to Growth in Early Reading Achievement: Quantitative Analysis*. Paper presented at National Reading Conference annual conference, Austin, TX.

U.S. Department of Education. (1998a). *Turn Around Schools*. Washington, DC: Author.

U. S. Department of Education. (1998b). *Implementing Schoolwide Programs: An Idea Book on Planning*. Washington, DC: Author.

U. S. Department of Education, National Center for Educational Statistics. (1999). *The NAEP 1998 Reading Report Card for the Nation and the States*. Washington, DC: U. S. Department of Education.

Yin, R.K. (1984). *Case Study Research: Design and Methods*. Beverly Hills, CA: Sage Publications.

ENDNOTES

1. This research was supported under the Educational Research and Development Centers Program, PR/Award Number R305R70004, as administered by the Office of Educational Research and Improvement, U.S. Department of Education. However, the comments to not necessarily represent the positions or policies of the National Institute of Student Achievement, Curriculum, and Assessment or the National Institute on Early Childhood Development, or the U.S. Department of Education, and you should not assume endorsement by the Federal Government.

2. Both Texas and California schools had two administrators; a principal and an assistant principal. However, one California school (CA 6) was operating with only one principal at the time of the study.

Beyond Practice
Follow-Up of a Collaborative Urban Teaching Experience

9.

Ann Liedel-Rice

Ann Liedel-Rice, Professor in Elementary Education at Slippery Rock University, is currently directing an Urban Student Teaching Program. Areas of interest consist of restructuring teacher education to include multicultural education throughout the curriculum and into student teaching assessment.

ABSTRACT

The purpose of this follow-up study was to determine the impact of a 16-week urban student teaching program on former participants in their second through sixth year of classroom teaching. Survey and interview results indicated that participants viewed their opportunity to work with urban students as one of their most meaningful educational experiences. Findings suggest that carefully structured programs have the potential of encouraging beginning teachers to select urban settings as their choice of employment and that an intensification of multicultural instruction throughout the entire pre-service program is a critical need.

Introduction

Efforts to reform teaching and learning challenge teacher education institutions to accept the responsibility of preparing reflective candidates capable of establishing supportive classroom environments and optimal, equitable learning experiences for urban, suburban and rural students. According to Banks, Cookson, Gay, Howley, Irvine, Nieto, Schofield, and Stephan (2001),

167

"Schools should ensure that all students have equitable opportunities to learn," (p. 198) . . . and teachers "must be knowledgeable about the social and cultural contexts of teaching and learning" (p. 197). Prospective teachers should not only be skilled in knowing how to make content meaningful (Knapp, Shields, & Turnbull, 1995) but, in teaching in classrooms that are becoming increasingly more diverse (Matczynski, Rogus, Lasley II, & Joseph, 2000). They must also be prepared to understand how outside forces affect the classroom learning environment. As Liston & Zeichner (1996) contend:

> Future teachers cannot, on their own solve the many societal issues confronting the schools, but they should certainly know what those issues are, have a sense of their own beliefs about those issues, and understand the many ways in which those issues will come alive within the school's walls (pp. 10–11).

Studies indicate that the majority of future teachers lack the perquisite attitudes and dispositions that would empower them to make content meaningful to students who are culturally different from themselves (Avery & Walker, 1993; Barry & Lechner, 1995; Gilbert, 1995; Larke, 1990; Schultz, Neyart & Reck, 1996; Su, 1996, 1997). Sleeter's examination (in press) of pre-service teachers' attitudes regarding diversity reported, "Although a large proportion of white pre-service students anticipate working with children of another cultural background, as a whole they bring very little cross-cultural background, knowledge and experience" (p. 4).

In contrast, Ladson-Billings (1991); Rios & Montecinos (1999) and Su (1996, 1997) indicate that teacher candidates of color tend to bring knowledge, cross-cultural experiences and a commitment to social justice. Additionally, undergraduate minority education students were found to view white teacher education programs as inadequate (Parker & Hoods, 1995). Yet, all pre-service candidates need preparation in educational strategies and learning theory and face the challenges of learning how to teach (Goodwin, 1997).

Educators for the 21st century must understand and take into account the impact of poverty as well as the increasing numbers of culturally diverse students (Ladson-Billings, 1999). Demographer Harold Hodgkinson (1995) reports the number of children in the United States under age six living in poverty rose from five million in 1987 to six million in 1992. As one can imagine, such statistics on poverty do not bode well for the education of impoverished children. Nieto (2002) argues, "The cultural differences of students and the negative perception of these differences in the larger society places students at risk . . . because they are simply not given the minimal resources with which to learn" (p. 54). Additionally, Payne (1998) affirms the importance of understanding the impact of poverty on instruction and achievement.

In the face of increased poverty and student diversity, Zimpher and Ashburn (1992) point out teacher candidates' resistance to teaching in urban schools. They assert, "Even among the eight percent who came from major urban settings to attend college, only 33 percent would have considered returning to those cities to teach" (p. 41). Clearly, teacher education programs are faced with the problem of freeing pre-service candidates from their parochialism and to provide experiences that are geared to preparing them to successfully teach in urban settings.

Although teacher educators are urged to critique their urban initiates, few studies can be found that analyze programs from a multicultural perspective (Gomez, 1996; Grant & Secada, 1990; Grant & Tate, 1995; Marsh, 1975). Guyton (2000) emphasizes that research efforts should "examine how what we do in our programs affects what teachers do in their classrooms" (p. 112). The restructuring of teacher preparation programs should be based on what our graduates can do, not what we hope they can do (Goodlad, 1990). The necessity for understanding the effect on pre-service teachers who learn to teach students of diverse backgrounds (Zeichner, 1996) is the incentive for conducting a follow-up study of former urban student teachers.

Program Description

Towards the goal of preparing teacher candidates to reach all students, Slippery Rock University, a rural institution serving a predominately white (92.3%) student population, has worked in collaboration for the past ten years with the Pittsburgh City School District in an effort to meet the demands of preparing teachers for a democratic, multicultural society, a requirement of the National Council for Accreditation of Teacher Education (NCATE) since 1978 (Gollnick, 1995). Carlow College, a private institution in inner-city Pittsburgh, collaborated with Slippery Rock by furnishing an educational and residential center for participants.

The program endorses the following goals: (a) to promote the achievement of students in urban schools; (b) to enable participants to embark on a reflective process in examining the "influence of culture on their teaching style and on the learning styles of students" (p. 69) as recommended by Gollnick (1992); and (c) to prepare participants in recognizing inequitable issues of class, race, gender and disability as advocated by Sleeter & Grant (1999).

Faculty interview (Haberman, 1987) and carefully select candidates. Although data consistently indicate that applicants bring a limited knowledge of multicultural education, cultural experiences, and fear of urban settings, high expectations are held for education majors who elect to student teach in the urban program. First, data are obtained regarding each candidate's "interactions with children and youth" (p. 36) as recommended by Haberman (1987). Additionally, background knowledge, maturity, dispositions towards culturally diverse populations, responsibility, flexibility, organization skills and the ability to work in collaboration with others are taken into account. Selected candidates are assigned to schools in cohorts based on their interests and certification areas. Moreover, an effort is made to assign a mentor who exhibits a positive rapport with urban students, demonstrates effective teaching skills, and affords the student teacher opportunities to execute a degree of autonomy and leadership.

This systematic, cross-cultural teacher training involves participants in the learning process through direct experiences in urban schools. They begin their inner-city experience with three days of preparation at Carlow College. A safe community atmosphere (Peck, 1987) is cultivated, as student teachers, along with the university facilitator, examine specific guidelines for student teaching within the framework of understanding the urban learner. Professional development workshops are conducted by successful teachers and/or community residents sustaining internal renewal (Bolin, 1987). More importantly, they are geared to develop participants' understandings of multicultural education. Cultural experiences with community centers beyond the school setting are provided to foster an understanding of the life experiences of urban students (Ladison-Billings, 1994).

Statement of the Problem

This study addressed the following questions:

1. In what types of schools have former urban student teachers obtained jobs?
2. What are former urban student teachers' perceptions of how well their urban experience prepared them for working with culturally and diverse student populations?
3. Are former urban student teachers still interested in teaching urban students?
4. What are former urban student teachers' understanding of multicultural education?
5. What are recommendations of former urban student teachers in preparing teachers for diverse student populations?

Methodology

All of the 118 research participants successfully completed the urban student teaching program and were in their second through sixth year of teaching/work experience. First, a letter of invitation to participate in the study and a survey was sent to 176 former urban student teachers to gather information pertaining to demographics, current job; type of school (urban, suburban or rural); percentage of diverse student populations, years of teaching; impact of program experiences; and recommendations for preparing preservice candidates.

The survey was returned by 118 of the 176 (67%) former urban student teachers. The respondent group included two African American males, 15 Caucasian males, one Latino American female, and 100 Caucasian females. Of the 118 who returned their survey, 93 have obtained jobs in education, 13 are in business, four are parenting, four are working in social services, three are working in technology, and one is in the military.

A second method of data gathering was observation and interviews. Each respondent's survey was examined for what was said about their current teaching situations in relation to the perceived benefits and deficiencies of the urban program. Participants were asked to identify their school as: urban, suburban or rural. They were also asked to estimate the percentage of non-white students in their school using the following categories: 75–100%; 50–74%; 25–49%; and 0–24%. Visits were ascertained primarily by geographic location and financial restraints. In addition, survey comments suggested data to investigate. For example, a third year teacher felt that the urban program didn't sufficiently prepare her. She acknowledged:

> The urban program gave me support for working with students of backgrounds different than my own. However, it did not fully prepare me for the Native American culture. I feel more emphasis should be taught in methods about cultures and the differences. . . . Classes need to be developed for presenting what is not appropriate in all cultures.

Initial contact for a visit to a respondent's classroom was made by phone. An effort was made to affirm a collegial relationship in examining what helped or didn't help during his/her urban experience. Details were discussed to facilitate taking pictures of students and interview procedures. Of the 20 teachers contacted only one refused. Apprehension was conveyed about what the researcher might ask administration regarding multicultural education. Finally, visits were made to: seven urban schools including four elementary schools, two middle schools and one secondary school; eight suburban schools including five elementary schools and two middle schools;

and four rural elementary schools in Arizona, Florida, Maryland, New Mexico, North Carolina, Ohio, and Pennsylvania.

A full day was spent observing each of the 19 former urban student teachers in their current teaching assignments. Field notes were made of room arrangement, decorations, instructional strategies, and most importantly, teacher-student interactions. Observations served as preparation for interviews, providing the researcher with an understanding of participants' responses in relation to their teaching situation. Interviews were conducted after school, providing an opportunity to establish rapport as well as a period of time for the respondent to reflect on his/her teaching assignment and urban experience (Costa & Garmston, 1994).

For the most part, interviews were semi-structured. The researcher used one question that required the respondent to choose from a set of responses to ensure more systematic data (Mishler, 1986). The open-ended, prepared questions were consistent with the survey, but remained open to alternative directions in which the responses directed the interview. Probes were used to elicit clarification and elaboration (Spradley, & McCurdy, 1972). The intent was to determine the importance former urban student teachers gave to their urban student teaching in relation to their current teaching, their interpretation of multicultural education, and recommendations for preparing pre-service teachers.

The theoretical framework utilized in analyzing the observations and interviews of former urban student teachers was drawn from Sleeter and Grant's (1999) typology. The following rubric was devised and utilized:

1. Business as Usual: Teacher indicates limited or no awareness of class, race, gender, or other differences. No specific plans for integrating multicultural education are shared (pp. 1–36).
2. Teaching the Exceptional and Culturally Different Approach: Teacher demonstrates or explains that the main purpose of instruction is to raise achievement scores or obtain a job. Content is made relevant to students' experiential background. Instruction is built on students' experiences and/or special classes are designed to provide success in school and the society (p. 38).
3. The Human Relations Approach: Teacher explains that the purpose of multicultural education is to foster positive relationships and promote students' self-esteem, demonstrates or explains a variety of activities geared to eliminate stereotyping, and uses cooperative learning as an instructional strategy (p. 111).
4. Single-Group Studies: Teacher explains that the purpose of multicultural education is to teach information about cultural groups. Instructional

activities include contributions and struggles of marginalized populations (p. 111).

5. The Multicultural Education Approach: Teacher explains how content is
made relevant to students' lives. She discusses how multicultural issues
are infused into the curriculum and utilizes critical/creative question
techniques and instructional strategies involving students in thinking
and working together (p. 153).

6. The Multicultural and Social Reconstructionist Approach: Teacher
explains how students are taught skills for social action in dealing with
their own lives and how she facilitates social action opportunities for
parents or community members in dealing with their own life circumstances. She describes how issues of inequity have been identified and
what social actions have been employed, utilizes strategies promoting
critical thinking and different points of view and facilitates experiences
in decision-making (p. 189).

In addition, semi-structured interviews were conducted with 15 building
principals, two assistant principals, and two mentors who offered to meet
with the researcher regarding their perceptions of former urban student
teachers. The interviews functioned as a form of triangulation seeking to
enhance validation (Mason, 1996). Data were examined surrounding four
major issues of participants' "classroom performance," "effect on their students," "contribution to the school/community," and evidence of "integrating multicultural issues" in their teaching. All interviews, ranging in length
from 60 to 90 minutes, were recorded, transcribed, and examined for
themes relating to goals of the study.

Survey Results

School settings showed that 36 former urban student teachers obtained jobs
in urban schools, 42 in suburban schools and 15 in rural schools. However,
these statistics are somewhat misleading since the majority of the placements of former urban student teachers were in ethnically diverse settings.
Fifty-three of the 93 respondents (57%) were working with ethnically
diverse student populations (See Table 1).

A majority (97%) of the respondents indicated that **their teaching experience in a culturally diverse setting** helped prepare them for working
with students in poverty, from diverse cultural backgrounds, or with special
needs populations. Respondents viewed student teaching placements in
very ethnically diverse settings, providing the candidate with the experience of being a minority, as more helpful than less diverse settings.

TABLE 1

School Settings of Former Urban Student Teachers

Urban Schools				
	Very Ethnically Diverse 70–100%	Less Ethnically Diverse 50–74%	Less Ethnically Diverse 25–49%	Least Ethnically Diverse 0–24%
Elem/EC	9	8	4	2
Middle	6	1	1	
Secondary	4		1	
Total: 36	19	9	6	2
Suburban Schools				
Elem/EC		3	4	21
Middle	1	3	3	4
Secondary			1	2
Total: 42	1	6	8	27
Rural Schools				
Elem/EC		1	1	6
Middle	1	1		2
Secondary				3
Total: 42	1	2	7	11
Summary				
Teaching: 93	Very Diverse (75–100)— Less Diverse (25–49): 53		Least Diverse (0–24): 40	
Related/Left: 25				
Total: 118				

Additionally, they viewed culturally diverse fieldwork settings as increasing their desire to obtain a job in an urban school by instilling confidence, heightening the willingness to relocate, solidifying the importance of understanding students' cultures, promoting the development of classroom management skills, developing critical thinking skills, providing the opportunity to learn how to work with teachers who reflect philosophies different than one's own, and expediting the process of obtaining a job. Most importantly, respondents indicated a strong awareness of the inequities in education between urban and suburban settings.

A majority (97%) felt that the **professional development** component of the urban program was beneficial. Learning to overcome one's intercultural deficits was seen as very challenging, but seminars and visits to community centers were cited as helpful in obtaining a different perspective on urban issues. Seminars in small groups were more beneficial than large groups. Respondents indicated that the supportive atmosphere encouraged them to deal with feelings of isolation and rejection that can come from working with cultures different from one's own.

Although 83% of respondents were **motivated to teach in urban schools**, 17% indicated that the work is too challenging, and that the political agendas of urban schools, the scarcity of basic instructional materials, lack of preparation for working with urban parents, and a shortage of full time positions creates a negative effect on motivation to teach in urban schools.

A majority of the respondents (99%) would **select the program again**. Comments indicated that the Urban Program experience prompted reflection on professional identity, cultivation of diversity, an awareness of inequity issues in society, and an interest in urban education.

Observation/Interview Results

This section presents data obtained through observations of respondents in their classroom settings and through interviews. This data led the researcher in determining that 15 of the 19 former urban student teachers (79%) indicated an ideology best characterized by Sleeter & Grant's (1999) Teaching the Exceptional and Culturally Different and Human Relations Approaches. In order to protect confidentiality, former urban student teachers' names are pseudonyms.

While preparing for classroom visits, the researcher did not request that teachers use any specific pedagogical strategy so it was surprising to see Leslie, a third year, seventh grade, math teacher who had been effective in utilizing cooperative learning as an urban student teacher standing at the front of the room facing her students who were sitting in rows. Speaking with a clear, enthusiastic voice, she demonstrated samples on the overhead, making sure each student was involved. Then, students were assigned partners to engage in talking as they worked. Ten minutes before class ended, Leslie presented clear rubrics for their homework assignment while she circulated around the room, making sure each student had understood the assignment. At the end of class, she positioned herself to respond to concerns or questions. During the follow-up interview, Leslie explained, "Cooperative learning is important. Now, we're learning how to work together . . . Come back in November and we'll be working in groups."

Lisa, a secondary special education teacher, was initiated into her school by colleagues telling her, "You probably won't make it through the first week!" However, at the time of the interview, she was successfully finishing her third year. She not only used cooperative learning, but also had obtained three grants for bringing technology into her classroom. These two teachers' final report showed their students stayed in school and progressed academically, resulting in promotion or graduation.

The teachers used a variety of creative instructional approaches in facilitating students in learning academic concepts. For example, Brad, a third year, second grade, suburban teacher, went beyond the single-correct answer approach by utilizing Howard Gardner's notion of "multiple intelligences" offering students opportunities to show their unique abilities. His principal proudly shared the class's high standardized test scores and reported that Brad's students laughed during the writing section saying, "This is easy."

Considerable accounts addressed disposition issues and/or special needs students. Kevin, a sixth year teacher, reported that he had offered to accept five children who were known to exhibit troubling behaviors. Not wanting to call attention to them, he teamed up with Ms. R., a special education teacher. Together they prepared all of Kevin's fourth graders to serve as teaching assistants in Ms. R's classroom. They read to the children, played games, reinforced skills, and provided attention to those needing help with putting on coats or holding a feeding tube. The fourth graders willingly took turns sacrificing their recess to help in Ms. R's room. Assisting the children during lunch and getting ready for dismissal served as a service-learning project. Kevin found that his students had learned to work cooperatively in his classroom as well as assisting in Ms. R.'s room. As a result, students completed class assignments and homework. His principal spoke positively of Kevin's ability to engage students in learning saying, "They are always totally immersed in whatever they happen to be working on." Then he added, "He has good rapport with parents, too."

Renee, a third year teacher, realizing that some teachers don't want to teach special needs students, offered to work with all of the third graders. She was exceptional in actively engaging them with an array of meaningful hands-on activities. Periodically, she used current events for helping her students realize how some groups of people are marginalized in our society. She wondered how she might bring in more multicultural issues and what parents might think.

Former urban student teachers at these two levels basically understood multicultural education as academic achievement and fostering positive relationships. They reported the use of multicultural books and activities that promoted self-esteem and less stereotypical attitudes. The variety and thoroughness of multicultural activities and teaching performances varied from celebrating cultural holidays to focusing on units of study. Cooperative learning was cited as widely used for facilitating academic success and fostering positive relationships.

MOVING TOWARDS TRANSFORMATIONAL AND SOCIAL ACTION APPROACHES

The behaviors and responses of four teachers suggested a movement towards transformation and social change. Julie, a fifth year teacher working in a suburban school, responded to the survey saying, "The county offered me a position in one of three schools. I selected the school that allowed me to teach sixth grade and follow the majority of my African American students who were bused to the suburban school."

Julie's change from an urban to a suburban school resulted in meeting head-on issues of racism among students and colleagues. Now, she was working with a combination of low and upper-middle class students. Observations and interviews indicated that Julie was intent on facilitating an equitable learning environment for all students. She integrated multicultural lessons into the curriculum. Julie recognized that many of her low-income students felt discouraged and she was empowering them in dealing with an oppressive situation.

Beth, a fifth-year middle school teacher, worked in a very diverse urban setting she called a "war zone." However, her keen sense of responsibility created a family atmosphere. A table in the center of the room was the focal point where students were encouraged to discuss issues of concern. She discussed the importance of understanding students' cultures and why teachers need to become involved with their students beyond the school. She was very proud that she had obtained a grant for developing an after-school program. She was grateful for her Urban Program involvement, but she was disappointed that her course work at Slippery Rock provided neither a solid background in multicultural education nor Spanish. Yet, she was comfortable in teaching Hispanic students and firm in her choice of urban teaching.

Donna, a second year, primary learning support teacher was thriving in a 98% African American inner-city school. Each day, she and a second grade teacher worked together to involve students in utilizing multicultural literature and the writing process. Children were excited to find out about the contributions of African Americans. Donna praised students for their cooperation in working together and enthusiastically introduced the activity, bringing out issues of inequity; for example, by using a book about Rosa Parks, she endeavored to help children see the value of working together to affect positive change. One student performed so well he was taken out of special education. Another student, a reluctant writer, began writing. In addition, Donna was establishing a strong connection with parents and the community.

John, a fifth-year teacher, taught sixth graders at a middle school of very diverse populations. He successfully built an alternative education program for students experiencing low test scores. John had high expectations and was successful in engaging his students in complex mathematical problems. As a result, his students were clearly showing academic progress. John generously gave of his time in supporting students, parents, and the school community. He realized issues troubling his students and initiated a counseling program geared to help them learn how to manage their anger and develop strategies for dealing with oppression. John was recognized by some of his white colleagues for knowing how to teach African American students.

What made Julie, Beth, Donna, and John stand out among 19 of the former urban student teachers? They (a) designed instructional activities to reflect the concerns and interests of their students (Grant, 1991); (b) involved students in decision making ; and (c) showed a willingness to pay the price of identifying with a more assertive educational position in opposing issues of racism or inequity. Their principals confirmed their dedication to their students, integrity in maintaining a learner-centered philosophical approach, and a commitment in working towards social structural equality.

BUSINESS AS USUAL

Sleeter & Grant (1999) warned, "Try to change individuals and things will quickly return to their old ways if the world they experience remains unchanged" (p. 191). This statement was represented clearly in two former urban student teachers who had obtained teaching positions in their home rural schools. Reflecting on how multicultural education was carried out in her school, one former participant said, "Very little." The second teacher responded by saying,

> "It's easy to push it aside because you don't have to deal with it. Even with Martin Luther King, I was going to push it aside, but, a Title I teacher offered to do something. It was great and the kids really enjoyed it. They didn't know who he was or why we celebrate that day."

Both teachers discussed the importance of the willingness to work with special needs and children of poverty, but their overall application of multicultural education was limited. The philosophical views of these two former participants seemed to fit Sleeter & Grant's (1999) group "Business As Usual" (pp. 1–36).

PRE-SERVICE PREPARATION IN MULTICULTURAL EDUCATION

In order to bring closure to the discussion of multiculturalism, the researcher asked, "How would you rate your overall pre-service preparation in multicultural education *prior* to the urban program: (a) Very Adequate; (b) Adequate; or (c) Not Adequate?" Responses varied and seemed to reflect each former urban student teacher's experiences and overall concern for multicultural education. For example, a fifth year suburban teacher in a school setting of ethnically diverse populations indicated that the urban program offered the opportunity to adapt lessons to students' learning styles. In reflecting on her methods versus the urban experience, she stated, "I think my professors provided a wealth of resources and information on various subjects . . . but I needed to learn how to teach different student populations. I definitely got that out of the urban program." Reflecting on her pre-service preparation in multicultural education, she concluded, "Without the urban experience, not adequate."

In summary, two former urban student teachers in suburban settings felt their preparation was very adequate and six former participants felt their overall preparation was basically adequate. Eleven of the former urban student teachers considered their preparation not adequate for teaching them how to infuse multicultural education throughout the curriculum. For example, a teacher in a rural school indicated that she wasn't sure how to talk to her predominantly white student population about diversity. Considering her overall preparation in knowing how to adapt multicultural education to her current teaching setting, she said, "I have to be honest. We are into a discussion about how to do multicultural education . . . and I don't know how."

RECOMMENDATIONS OF FORMER URBAN STUDENT TEACHERS

The survey and onsite visits produced a list of approximately 130 recommendations for the preparation of teachers. In order to make the list more manageable, the 118 surveys were reviewed for clusters of similarity. Transcribed interviews were analyzed and combined with survey clusters. Ten suggestions are as follows:

1. Pre-service teachers should have the opportunity to work under the direction of a minority teacher and participate in workshops and/or visits to urban community centers conducted by minority educators;
2. provide frequent and early exposure to urban schools and communities;
3. provide preparation in working with urban parents;
4. provide additional course work in multicultural education;
5. require more background in history, linking it with urban classrooms;
6. provide course work on cultures, beliefs, religions, and customs, teaching what is offensive to different groups;
7. teach how to deal with hate groups;
8. prepare teachers with a solid foundation in multicultural literature and available resources;
9. require course work in special education, foreign languages and classroom management; and
10. extend the urban student teaching experience beyond sixteen weeks.

Ladson-Billings's (2001) study of pre-service candidates who aspire to teach poor children of color reported similar recommendations for preparing teachers for diverse populations.

Discussion

The purpose of this study was to investigate the perceptions of former urban student teachers in their second through sixth year of teaching. All respondents had (a) chosen to student teach in inner-city schools, (b) agreed to participate in professional development experiences beyond the traditional student teaching program, and (c) were selected by the faculty as showing potential for succeeding in urban schools.

Findings generally support the position of Haberman, (1996) who argues that candidates should be recruited and selected for urban settings. In the program studied, seven of the 19 respondents interviewed were working in very diverse settings (75-100%). Of those, six indicated that the urban program gave them the confidence to select an urban setting as their choice of employment. All of the six respondents who were working in less diverse settings (50–74%) indicated that the urban program is what initially prepared them to work with students whose cultures and backgrounds differed from their own.

Seminars and cultural visits geared to helping participants relate to students and parents whose cultures and life styles differed from their own were cited as critical components in becoming more confident in working with diverse student populations. Zeichner (1996) pointed out similar findings.

Liberman & Miller (2000) found that professional development providing teachers with a sense of belonging to a community had an impact on the way teachers thought about learning. A fifth year former urban student teacher, in a very diverse setting, supported this recommendation and reported that her supportive classroom environment modeled her student teaching seminars. Additional respondents in this study readily expressed that professional development seminars that started with a prompt where student teachers' issues were first examined and followed with an interactive presentation by an urban educator were helpful in maintaining self-esteem. More importantly, they stimulated reflections that resulted in personal behavioral changes. Zeichner, (1995) made similar arguments for utilizing students' concerns as a forum for discussion.

Ladson-Billings (2001) supported the importance of conducting seminars away from the student teachers' assigned schools, giving students the opportunity to say what was on their minds in an environment free of criticism. In contrast, Liberman & Miller (2000) argued that pre-service teachers shouldn't be isolated from the professional development of experienced teachers.

Former urban student teachers reported that seminars and workshops on instructional strategies conducted by successful practitioners were reported as beneficial and problematic. Although the professional development component supported the research of Ladson-Billings (1994) and Shade (1994), former participants indicated that creative techniques were in conflict with placements in schools that adhered to a strict, text-based curriculum.

While beginning teachers need to be caring, competent problem-solvers and risk-takers in meeting the needs of diverse student populations, ten former urban student teachers cited institutional bureaucracies as limiting the opportunities for teaching and learning. Weiner's (1993) critical study of urban schools noted: "Urban teachers confront the greatest diversity of student needs, but the conditions in urban schools severely limit individualization" (p. 110).

Early recognition of institutional constraints and/or current teaching experiences of seven former student teachers working in very diverse settings helped prepare them for urban settings. This data supported the research of Cochran-Smith (1991) which examined the effects of preparing teachers to teach against the system. Yet, an introduction to urban systems did not encourage all former urban students to select an urban setting for employment. Three former student teachers, working in least diverse settings, indicated a desire to work with culturally diverse student populations, but they did not want to deal with the curriculum restrictions of urban settings.

Respondents' recommendations for preparing teachers for urban schools indicated a limited theoretical preparation in multicultural content and classroom experiences in culturally, diverse settings. Former urban student teachers who were working with either Native American or Hispanic populations indicated a lack of pertinent background knowledge, a problem recognized by the research of Smith, (1998) in preparing teacher candidates in the essential elements of culture.

Gay (2001) emphasized, "If more diverse students are to achieve higher levels of school success," more will be demanded of teachers "than simply being aware, respectful, and tolerant of cultural diversity" (p. 24). For the most part, research participants of this study indicated a human relations approach in the application of principles of multicultural education as described by Sleeter & Grant (1999). Only four of the 19 former urban student teachers interviewed indicated a movement toward transformation and social action approaches (Sleeter & Grant, 1999). All four former urban student teachers called attention to issues regarding the marginalization of poor students and students of color within school systems.

Finally, the outcomes of this study indicated that carefully structured, supportive urban programs have the potential of encouraging beginning teachers to select urban settings as their choice of employment and as Gomez (1996) found "begins the critical self-inquiry demanded if perspective teachers are to successfully teach diverse learners" (p. 125).

Implications for Teacher Education

The results of this self-study indicated that former urban student teachers viewed their opportunity to work in urban schools as one of their most meaningful educational experiences during their undergraduate work, but they realized they had a limited background in multicultural content. Data suggested that teacher candidates need a solid background in the principles of multicultural education emphasizing social justice and the opportunity to connect theory with classroom practice throughout their pre-service preparation (Murrell & Diez, 1997).

Teacher education curriculum must be guided by a conceptual framework that "infuses the concepts of democracy and multicultural advocacy into student teaching assessment" (Vavrus, 1999, p. 6).

Teacher education programs, including institutions located in predominantly white settings, should adhere to the NCATE 2000 standards in preparing teacher candidates for teaching all students. Pre-service candidates should be prepared to implement the principles of multicultural education for all student populations (Banks, 1999). For Haberman (1987) warns, "Our system of education will not be judged on how well we do in rural and suburban America, but on how well we do in the urban areas" (p. 1).

Collaborative initiatives between classroom teachers and university instructors need to develop research based programs in preparing candidates for urban schools and for teaching from a multicultural perspective in urban, suburban and rural schools. Follow-up studies should be conducted to determine successful teachers' level of understanding and application of what was learned or not learned (Sleeter, in press). Reform efforts in preparing pre-service candidates should consistently address the structures of teacher education within the context of multicultural education (Ladson-Billings, 1995).

REFERENCES

Avery, P.G. & Walker, C. (1993). Prospective Teachers' Perceptions of Ethnic and Gender Differences in Academic Achievement. *Journal of Teacher Education, 44*(1), 27–37.

Banks, J. A., Cookson, P., Gay, G., Hawley, W.D., Irvine, J.J., Nieto, S., Ward, J. Schofield, J. W., and Stephan, W.G. (2001). Diversity Within Unity: Essential Principles for Teaching and Learning in a Multicultural Society. *Phi Delta Kappan, 83*(3), 196–203.

Banks, J. A. (1999). *An Introduction to Multicultural Education* (2nd Ed.). Boston: Allyn & Bacon.

Barry, N. H. & Lechner, J.V. (1995). Pre-Service Teachers' Attitudes about and Awareness of Multicultural Teaching and Learning. *Teaching and Teacher Education, 11*(2), 149–161.

Bolin, F. S. (1987). Reassessment and Renewal in Teaching. In F. S. Bolin & J.M. Falk (Eds.), *Teacher Renewal* (pp. 6–16). New York: Teachers College Press.

Cochran-Smith, M. (1991). Learning to Teach against the Grain. *Harvard Educational Review, 61*(3), 279–310.

Costa, A. & Garmston, R. (1994). *Cognitive Coaching: A Foundation for Renaissance Schools.* Norwood, MA: Christopher-Gordon Publishers.

Gay, G. (2001). Effective Multicultural Teaching Practices. In C. F. Diaz (Ed.). *Multicultural Education for the 21st Century* (pp. 23–41). New York: Longman.

Gilbert, S.L. (1995). Perspectives of Rural Prospective Teachers toward Teaching in Urban Schools. *Urban Education, 30*(3), 290–306.

Gollnick, D. (1995). National and State Initiatives for Multicultural Education. In J. Banks & C.A.Banks (Eds.) *Handbook of Research on Multicultural Education* (pp. 44–64). New York: Macmillan.

Gollnick, D. (1992). Understanding the Dynamics of Race, Class and Gender. In M. Dillworth (Ed). *Diversity in Teacher Education* (pp. 63–78). San Francisco: Jossey-Bass.

Gomez, M.L. (1996). Prospective Teachers' Perspectives on Teaching "Other People's Children." In K. Zeichner, S. Melnick, & M.L. Gomez (Eds.). *Currents of Reform in Pre-Service Teacher Education* (pp. 109–132). New York: Teachers College Press.

Goodlad, J. (1990). *Teachers for Our Nation's Schools.* San Francisco: Jossey Bass Publishers.

Goodwin, A.L. (1997). Multicultural Stories. *Urban Education, 32*(1), pp. 117–148.

Grant, C.A. (1991). Culture and Teaching: What Do Teachers Need to Know? In M. Kennedy (Ed.), *Teaching Academic Subjects to Diverse Learners* (pp. 237–255). New York: Teachers College Press.

Grant, C.A. & Secada, W.G. (1990). Preparing Teachers for Diversity. In W.R. Houston & J. Sikula (Eds.), *Handbook of Research on Teacher Education* (pp. 403–422). New York: Macmillan Publishing Company.

Grant, C. & Tate (1995). Multicultural Education through the Lens of Multicultural Education Literature. In J. Banks (Ed.) *Handbook of Research on Multicultural Education* (pp. 145–166). New York: Macmillan Publishing Company.

Guyton, E. (2000). Social Justice in Teacher Education. *The Educational Forum,* (64), 108–114.

Haberman, M. (1987). *Recruiting and Selecting Teachers for Urban Schools.* New York: ERIC Clearinghouse on Urban Education, Institute for Urban and Minority Education.

Haberman, M. (1996). Selecting and Preparing Culturally Competent Teachers for Urban Schools. In J. Sikula, T.J. Buttery & E. Guyton (Eds.) *Handbook of Research on Teacher Education* (2nd ed., pp. 747–760). New York: Macmillan.

Hodgkinson, H. (1995). What Should We Call People? Race, Class, and the Census for 2000. *Phi Delta Kappan, 77*(2), 173–179.

Knapp, M. S., Shields, P.M. & Turnbull, B.J. (1995). Academy Challenge in High-Poverty Classrooms. *Phi Delta Kappan, 76*(10), 770–776.

Ladson-Billings, G. (1991). Beyond Multicultural Illiteracy. *Journal of Negro Education, 60*(2), 147–157.

Ladson-Billings, G. (2001). *Crossing Over to Canaan: The Journey of New Teachers in Diverse Classrooms.* San Francisco: Jossey-Bass Publishers.

Ladson-Billings, G. (1995). Multicultural Teacher Education: Research, Practice and Policy. In J. A. Banks & C. A. Banks (Eds.), *Handbook of Research of Multicultural Education* (pp. 747–759). New York: Macmillan.

Ladson-Billings, G. (1999). Preparing Teachers for Diversity. In L. Darling-Hammond & G. Sykes (Eds.) *Teaching As The Learning Profession* (pp. 86–123). San Francisco: Jossey-Bass.

Ladson-Billings, G. (1994). *The Dreamkeepers: Successful Teachers of African American Children.* San Francisco: Jossey-Bass Publishers.

Larke, P. J. (1990). Cultural Diversity Awareness Inventory: Assessing the Sensitivity of Pre-Service Teachers. *Action in Teacher Education, 12*(3), 23–30.

Lieberman, A. & Miller, L. (2000). Teaching and Teacher Development: A New Synthesis for a New Century. In R.S. Brandt (Ed.) *Education in a New Era* (pp. 47–66). Virginia: Association for Supervision and Curriculum Development.

Liston, D. & Zeichner, K. (1996). *Culture and Teaching.* New Jersey: Lawrence Erlbaum Associates.

Mason, J. (1996). *Qualitative Researching.* London: Sage Publications.

Matczynski, T., Rogus, J., Lasley, T. and Joseph, E. (2000). Culturally Relevant Instruction: Using Traditional and Progressive Strategies in Urban Schools. *The Educational Forum*, (64), 350–357.

Marsh, D.D. (1975). An Evaluation of Sixth Cycle Teacher Corps Graduates. *Journal of Teacher Education, 26*(2), 139–140.

Mishler, E.G. (1986). *Research Interviewing.* Cambridge, MA: Harvard University Press.

Murrell, P. J. & Diez, M. (1997). A Model Program or Educating Teachers for Diversity. In J. E. King, E. R. Hollins & W. C. Haymon (Eds.), *Preparing Teachers for Cultural Diversity* (pp. 113–128). New York: Teachers College Press.

Nieto, N. (2002). *Language, Culture and Teaching: Critical Perspectives for a New Century.* New Jersey: Lawrence Erlbaum Associates, Publishers.

Parker, L. & Hood, S. (1995). Minority Students vs. Majority Faculty and Administrators in Teacher Education: Perspectives on the Clash of Cultures. *The Urban Review, 27*(2), 159–174.

Payne, R.K. (1998) *A Framework for Understanding Poverty.* Highlands, TX: RFT Publishing Co.

Peck. S. (1987). *The Different Drum: Community and Peace.* New York: Touchstone Rockfeller Center.

Rios, F. & Montecinos, C. (1999). Advocating Social Justice and Cultural Affirmation. *Equity & Excellence in Education, 32*(3), 66–77.

Schultz, E.I., Neyhart, K. & Reck, U.M. (1996). Swimming Against the Tide: A Study of Prospective Teachers' Attitudes Regarding Cultural Diversity and Urban Teaching. *Western Journal of Black Studies, 20*(1), 1–7.

Shade, B.J. (1994). Understanding the African American Learner. In E. R. Hollins, J. E. King, & W. Hayman (Eds.), *Teaching Diverse Populations Formulating a Knowledge Base* (pp. 175–189). Albany: State University of New York Press.

Sleeter, C. (in press). Epistemological Diversity in Research on Pre-Service Teacher Preparation for Historically Underserved Children. In W. Seceda, (Ed.), *Review of Research in Education,* Washington, DC: American Education Research Association.

Sleeter, C. & Grant, C. (1999). *Making Choices for Multicultural Education: Five Approaches to Race, Class, and Gender* (3rd ed.). Columbus, Ohio: Merrill.

Spradley, J.P. and McCurdy, D.W. (1972). *The Cultural Experience.* Chicago, IL: Science Research Associates.

Smith, P. G. (1998). *Common Sense about Uncommon Knowledge: The Knowledge Bases for Diversity.* Washington, DC: American Association of Colleges of Teacher Education Publications.

Su, Z. (1996). Why Teach: Profiles and Entry Perspectives of Minority Students as Becoming Teachers. *Journal of Research and Development in Education, 29*(3), 117–133.

Su, Z. (1997). Teaching as a Profession and as a Career: Minority Candidates' Perspectives. *Teaching and Teacher Education, 13*(3), 325–40.

Vavrus, M. (1999). *Pre-Service Teacher Performance Assessment During Student Teaching: Consequences and Pitfalls.* Paper presented at the National Association of State Directors of Teacher Education & Certification National Symposium, Bellevue, Washington D.C.

Weiner, L. (1993). *Preparing Teachers for Urban Schools.* New York: Teachers College Press.

Zeichner, I. (1996). Educating Teachers for Cultural Diversity. In K. Zeichner, S. Melnick M.L.Gomez (Eds.), *Currents of Reform in Pre-Service Teacher Education* (pp. 133–175). New York: Teachers College.

Zeichner, K. (1995). Reflections of a teacher educator working for social change. In. T. Russell & F.S.A.J. Korthagen (Eds.), *Teachers Who Teach Teachers: Reflection on Teacher Education* (pp. 11–24). London: Falmer Press.

Zimpher, N. & Ashburn, E. (1992). Countering parochialism in teacher candidates. In M. E. Dilworth (Ed.), *Diversity in Teacher Education* (pp. 40–62). San Francisco: Jossey-Base Publishers.

Continuing the Dialogue on Teachers for and Teachers in Culturally Diverse Schools

Edwina Battle Vold and Jyotsna Pattnaik

Synthesis and Implications

The three research studies in this section have implications for how we prepare teachers for diverse student populations. The studies are distinctly different, however, there is a similar concern that surfaces and some related themes. The concern centers around the extent to which research can improve practice whether in teacher education or in programs in schools. In other words how does what we know about how teachers teach and what students learn affect our practices in schools with diverse student populations? The recurring themes are: diversity, including poor and limited English proficient children, collaboration, and systemic reform. We synthesize the research studies as they relate to the three themes.

High Poverty Schools

Within the theme of diversity, there is the issue of class. More explicitly, there are many children who are not achieving in schools who are poor and socially disenfranchised. So, with regard to teaching and learning and children of poverty, we revisit a classic research study of the 1970s by Ray C. Rist on *Student Social Class and Teacher Expectations: The Self-Fulfilling Prophecy in Ghetto Education* (reprinted in Rist, 2000). In this study, Rist describes how, for the one class of children he observed, their public school not only mirrored the class system of the larger society, but also actively contributed to maintain the status quo. In 2000, Harvard Education Review reprinted the research study with an introduction by Rist. In his introduc-

189

tion thirty years later, Rist continues to highlight the issues of color and class inequality in American society and education in America. He states:

> The basic challenge is that there is a profound disconnect between the rhetoric and the reality of American society for those on the bottom rung of the economic ladder. While the rhetoric is that of opportunity (be it through education, training, trickle-down economic growth, urban revitalization, etc.) the reality for those in the lowest 20 percent quintile of economic resources is quite different. Indeed, those in this bottom 20 percent have in the past thirty years actually lost ground to the rest of society, (p. 263) . . . The sobering reality is that when it comes to both color and class, U.S. schools tend to conform much more to the contours of American society than they transform it (p. 260).

The challenge by Rist is not unfounded as reported in M. Adler's study on *Successful Reading Achievement in 'Beat the Odds' Schools*. However, in Adler's study there is some hope especially for the improvement in reading found in 'high poverty,' 'beat the odds' schools in America. The purpose of the study, which took place in school districts in three different states, was to define the characteristics that distinguish high-poverty/high-achieving schools from high-poverty/low-achieving schools. What the study revealed was that there were distinct structural policies and practices that were in place in all of the high-poverty/high-achieving schools. These schools demonstrated characteristics such as high expectations of children, effective leadership, teacher/team collaboration and on-going professional development. It was important to note that in the three schools with large percentages of limited English proficient (LEP) children, the same characteristics of success in teaching children to read were present. There were also specific examples of teacher behavior and practices that reflected the identified characteristics.

The results of this study echo much of the research on effective schools and specific programs and projects. The implications from this study are that the results of this research can be translated into workable teacher education programs; and that schools with the characteristics of the schools in the study can help children in high-poverty areas 'beat the odds' and become successful readers. The research offers those in teacher education specific practices that can reform our reading methods and foundation courses. The research further supports the underlying theme that posits that observing and participating in naturalistic 'beat-the-odds' settings, can generate solutions regarding the dynamics of power and privilege that nurture, sustain and legitimate inequities (Weis & Fine, 1993).

The researcher clearly states, however, that for poor, language-minority, and/or dialect-speaking children growing up in urban environments and attending low-performing schools, the odds of successful achievement are not in their favor. Though poverty is not the sole indicator of reading difficulties, it contributes when combined with ineffective teachers who 'mouth' the rhetoric and under-funded programs that fail to take into consideration the vast and complex needs of the poor.

Collaboration

In their simplest form, school-university partnerships are organized collaboratives that bring university and public school teachers together to promote more effective preparation of pre-service teachers and, at the same time, renew conditions and curricula in the public schools. In some partnerships, as in the English Language Learning (ELL) program described in the Tate, Anstrom and Sanchez study, parents are included as official partners, in others social agencies and businesses are participants.

According to Osguthorage, Harris, Harris, & Black (1995) partner schools are selected sites where collaborative programs are put into practice. These authors relate that although no two partner schools are completely alike, all school/university partnerships appear to have been formed with two broad general goals; first, to strengthen the preparation of teachers and, second, to renew K–12 education. They further state that to advance these goals, four basic areas of partnership activity have been designated—all aimed at increasing student learning. The areas are:

1. Educator preparation: collaboration between partners to ensure that those entering the profession are prepared to serve all students effectively.
2. Professional development: collaboration between partners to provide opportunities for teachers to strengthen their ability to contribute to the students they serve.
3. Curriculum development: collaboration between partners to improve the education and school experience of all students.
4. Research and inquiry: collaboration between partners to raise questions and conduct research that will promote educational renewal at both the school and the university (pp. 2–3).

There are expectations of partner schools that should be taken into consideration when we design programs and when we do collaborative evaluation. They include: open communication, working to provide equity and excellence for all students and for all other members of the collaborative institutions; understanding the learning needs of all students and being committed to helping all children learn; collaborating in professional development to link theory, research and practice; and continuous engagement in reflective practice (critical inquiry) as a means of generating continuous improvement in teaching and learning for children and for pre-service teachers (Clark, 1995).

In the study by Tate, Anstrom and Sanchez, *Cooperating Teachers: The Challenges in Their Dual Roles as Mentors of Teachers Interns and Teachers of English Language Learners,* there is evidence of the effect of collaboration with university faculty and teachers and parents. While the cooperating teachers are coping with dual roles in providing professional development experiences for teacher candidates and providing learning experiences that accommodate the needs of ELL students, they have found a way in their focus groups to share with teacher education faculty ways that they can be more helpful. This communication process brought out concerns about cultural factors often misunderstood by interns and the lack of resources for ELL students needed by teachers especially in mainstream classrooms. The implication for teacher education under-scores the need to validate the expertise of cooperating teachers in practices that support the various theories presented in campus coursework.

The limited English proficient (LEP) population is the fastest growing in the United States. Although estimates of how many LEP or ELL children and adolescents are now in the schools vary, it is probable that almost eight million American youngsters have a non-English background, either because they were born elsewhere or because they grew up in a home in which another language was spoken. Unfortunately, many LEP students do poorly in school because they are taught by monolingual English-speaking teachers and more will continue to do poorly unless we can prepare a cadre of graduates who are knowledgeable and skilled in teaching the LEP or ELL children who are populating our schools (Grossman, 1995).

Systemic Reform

Besides seminars and content/method courses, clinical experiences in cross-cultural settings also provide prospective teachers with a concrete experience of the dynamics of racism, class elitism and gender bias at both the individual and society/institutional levels. The need for field experiences in culturally diverse schools has been emphasized by the Holmes Group (1990), as well as NCATE (1992, 1995) and validated by research findings from studies by Fuller & Abler (1987), Larke (1990), Vold (1994) and Vold, Zhang, Brown, and Kolakowski (1998) and a comparative study by Cooper, Beare & Therman (1990).

In the follow up study by Ann Liedel-Rice, *Beyond Practice: Follow-Up of a Collaborative Urban Teaching Experience,* there are indications that the urban experiences of the graduates were beneficial and were factors in their selection of job placements. She describes an undergraduate teacher education program that is successful mainly because of the collaboration between the university, the school district and a private college that served as 'safe' housing.

Liedel-Rice skillfully used the Sleeter and Grant typology in analyzing the observations and interviews of the nineteen former urban student teachers. This typology provided a wealth of information on the former students' understanding of multicultural education. While a majority of the nineteen former student teachers seemed to fall within the Human Relations Approach and four were moving toward the Transformation and Social Action Approach, there were some who reverted back to 'business as usual' —teaching as they were taught.

Clearly, the urban student teaching experience was an 'optional extra' (Phuntsog, 1995), though a successful experience for some in the teacher preparation program. Optional extras often do not lead to significant results since successful multicultural preparation warrants restructuring of the total organization framework (Gollnick, 1992). This concern for a more systemic approach to preparing teachers for urban schools with its diverse student populations is evidenced in the reflections of the former student teachers who now teach in different schools, including urban, rural and suburbia. In her summary, the researcher posits that 'optional extras' like the urban student teaching experience are not enough; that university supervisors and cooperating teachers need to engage in collaborative professional development to increase their knowledge of the principles of multicultural education in order to mentor teacher candidates beyond a basic human-relations approach.

Summary and Implications

There are implications from the title of this section "Educators Working in Diverse Schools: Linking Colleges of Education and Public Schools." One institution (College of Education) cannot prepare teachers for diversity without cooperating teachers and administrators in schools. One institution (the school) cannot be expected to create multicultural learning environments that respond to the needs of diverse student populations, including America's poorest without joint research efforts of teacher educators and theorists. In fact, the themes that we believe permeate all of the research studies, help the reader to focus on ways to make a difference in the way we prepare teachers. The same themes are essential for school reform. The research studies remind us of what we know works. However, the challenge is to have the courage to do what is morally and ethically our responsibility—to prepare the most effective teacher who will work in diverse school settings—and leave no child behind.

REFERENCES

Cooper, A. B., Beare, P., & Therman, J. (1990). Preparing Teachers for Diversity: A Comparison of Student Teaching Experiences in Minnesota and South Texas. *Action in Teacher Education, 12*(3), 1–4.

Clark, R. E. (1995). Evaluating Partner Schools. In R. T. Osguthorpe, R. C. Harris, M. F. Harris, & S. Black (Eds.). *Partner Schools: Centers for Educational Renewal* (pp. 238–146). San Francisco: Jossey-Bass Publishers.

Fuller, M., & Ahler, J. (1987). Multicultural Education and the Monocultural Student: A Case Study. *Action in Teacher Education, 9*(3), 253–264.

Gollnick, D. (1992). Understanding the Dynamics of Race, Class, and Gender. In M. E. Dilworth (Ed.). *Diversity in Teacher Education* (pp. 63–78). San Francisco: Jossey-Bass.

Grossman, H. (1995). *Teaching in Diverse Society.* Boston, MA: Allyn & Bacon.

Holmes Group Forum. (1990). *Research on Cultural Diversity, 6*(2), 9.

Larke, P. J. (1990). Cultural Diversity Awareness Inventory: Assessing the Sensitivity of Pre-Service Teachers. *Action in Teacher Education, 12*(3), 23–29.

National Council for Accreditation of Teacher Education (1995). *Quality Assurance for the Teaching Profession.* Washington, D.C.

Osguthorpe, R. T., Harris, M. F. & Black, S. (Eds.) (1995). *Partner Schools: Centers for Educational Renewal.* San Francisco: Jossey-Bass Publishers.

Phuntsog, N. (1995). Teacher Educators' Perceptions of the Importance of Multicultural Education in the Preparation of Elementary Teachers. *Equity & Excellence in Education, 28*(1), 10–14.

Rist, R. C. (2000). Student Social Class and Teacher Expectations: The Self-Fulfilling Prophecy in Ghetto Education. *Harvard Educational Review, 70*(3), 257–301. (Original work published 1970.)

Sleeter, C. E. & Grant, C. A. (1988). *Making Choices for Multicultural Education: Five Approaches to Race, Class and Gender.* Columbus, OH: Merrill.

Vold, L. A. (1994). A Study of the Relationship between Student Attitudes toward Urban Student Teaching and First Job Preferences. *SRATE Journal, 3*(1), 48–54.

Vold, L. A., Zhang, M., Brown, I. and Kolakowski, M. (1998, February). *Silk Purses from Sow's Ears or Yes Mother, European-American Students from Rural Areas and Small Towns can be Successful Urban Teachers.* Paper presented at the AACTE conference, New Orleans, LA.

Weis, L. & Fine, M. (1993). *Beyond Silenced Voices: Class, Race and Gender in United States Schools.* New York: State University of NY Press.